Fundamentals
of
OpenStack

By
Vishal Shukla

Copyright © 2014 by:Vishal Shukla

Published by
Vishal Shukla

ISBN: 1-4948-2759-X
ISBN-13: 9781494827595

Library of Congress Control Number: 2014902523
CreateSpace Indepent Publishing Platform, North Charleston, SC

Preface

Accelerated growth of data and diverse user base lead to the explosive growth of a phenomenon called Cloud. For the past few years many companies have been trying to come up with their own solutions on how the data center fabrics can be made and managed. The quest for an ultimate solution and standardization is still going on.

With time, data centers are also changing with every component moving towards "Software defined" in nature, which essentially means that hardware should be treated as a commodity and all logic should be in the centralized controller. The software defined movement is the need of the market right now – because data centers cannot be bottlenecked by vendor specific hardware which costs a fortune to install and maintain.

With Cloud expanding and data centers moving toward commodity hardware, there was an imminent need for an open standard based Cloud operating system, a stack which can run on any hardware, open enough to integrate multiple concepts and flexible enough for any vendor. Given these targets, OpenStack is the best.

The book flow is more of interactive rather textual & it is meant for educational purpose. The scope of this book is to discuss OpenStack and its modules from the conceptual angle. This book is meant for development engineers, system engineers, administrators, application developers, technical sales/ marketing and business executives who want to understand OpenStack end-to-end without going into hands-on configuration details.

This book covers details of all OpenStack modules based on Grizzly release. A brief chapter for Havana release has also been added which talks about Heat and Ceilometer. This book goes into details of components, and step-by-step working of each module.

This book does not cover any commands for installing OpenStack, any debugging commands, any hands-on information on the OpenStack system.

Acknowledgement

I am extremely grateful to my friends and colleagues who helped me by reviewing this book multiple times. Without their help this book would not have been possible. I would also like to thank Nitin Huralikuppi for supporting me on OpenStack setups.

A big thanks to my wife, son and extended family; each one of them helped me to write this book by accepting my long absences as I worked on the manuscript.

I dedicate this book to my parents, Kusum Shukla and the late P.N. Shukla, who have always been a source of inspiration and guidance for me.

Table of Content

- Characteristics of Nova
- Components of Nova
- Nova-API
- Nova-scheduler
- Nova-db
- Nova-conductor
- Nova-queue
- Nova-compute

- Image as a Service
- Overview of Glance
- Glance components
- Glance Architecture

- Cinder - Volume as a Service (Block)
- Characteristics of Cinder
- Components of Cinder

- Storage as a Service (Object)
- Overview of Swift
- Components & Concepts of Swift
- Architecture of Swift

- Neutron – Network as a Service
- Components of Neutron – Networking as a Service:
- Other Concepts
- Networking Architecture of OpenStack

- Multi-node OpenStack configuration using PackStack with Flat networking

Chapter -1 | Cloud

Cloud

To start with, there is no technology yet to store data and compute in real Clouds. The Clouds we refer are actually huge data centers storing billions of bytes of data and doing computations on that data. The customer does not know where the data centers are, and probably no one knows where a particular data is (and will be) stored and computed – so from the customer's point of view, where is the data storage and computation happening? It's happening somewhere in the air, but where exactly? In the Cloud.

Figure 1.1

Cloud refers to a distributed set of IT (Hardware/Software) resources which can be provisioned remotely giving a seamless access to the resources. These IT resources could include physical servers, virtual servers, storage devices, networking devices, services and software programs.

A group of these IT resources which could be present remotely at different locations but working together to service the needs of the company can be referred to as a Cloud.

The set of IT resources referred to as Cloud which a company uses is provided by an entity known as Cloud Provider. The company leveraging these resources is known as Cloud Consumer.

There are many ways of how a customer looks at Cloud. There are many customers who have their own Cloud, and some smaller customers rent the Cloud. Whether it's rented or in-house, the basics of a Cloud remain the same.

Characteristics of Cloud

Figure 1.2 gives a quick look into what all is essential about the Cloud. The following is a short explanation for those essential variables.

- On-demand Usage – Based on the requirements of the customer, the Cloud resources can be provisioned. The usage of the resources can be controlled, based on the need.

- Multi-tenancy – The Cloud can serve multiple customers or tenants where the data and information of each customer is maintained separately from the other. The resources can be assigned to different tenants with virtualization playing a key role.

- Elasticity – Elasticity is the ability of the Cloud to scale the resources based on the need of the customer or provider. The aim of Cloud Providers is to scale by putting more and more hardware and letting the Cloud operating system take charge of that hardware (rather than the Cloud admin trying to manually put it in resource list). The Cloud operating system will be more elastic when it will have more room to expand (by having more resources). This is one of the core features of the Cloud.

- High speed Accessibility – As defined, Cloud is a set of remote resources which can be provisioned by the application remotely. The Cloud being remote and distributed in nature, it makes accessibility a crucial variable. The Cloud is designed with high-speed accessibility as one core requirement.

- Tools for Billing – The services which a Cloud provides to customers should be measurable and there should be a tool inbuilt in the Cloud to measure the amount of compute, storage and network services which have been provided to the customer.

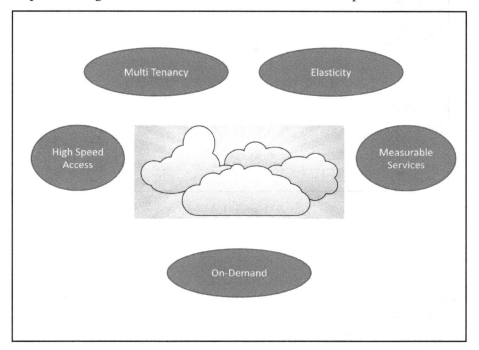

Figure 1.2
Cloud Essentials

Types of Cloud Deployments

Figure 1.3 gives a snapshot of the three types of Cloud deployment models. There are two companies shown in the example – Company-A and Company-B; and based on those the deployment usage is shown for three types of Cloud deployments

- Public Clouds

- Private Clouds

- Hybrid Clouds

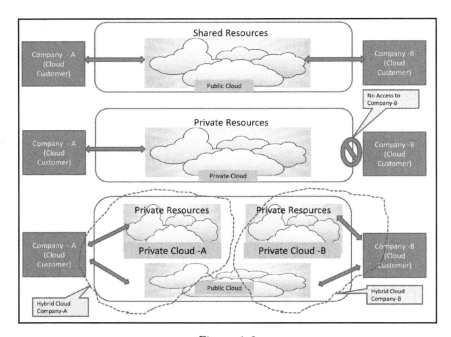

Figure 1.3
Cloud Deployment Models

Public Clouds

Public Cloud environment is completely owned by the company providing Cloud services. The Cloud users/customer does not own any infrastructure, whether hardware, software or anything else. The Cloud Provider leases the Cloud to the users based on their requirement and Scale. The Cloud Provider designs, manages, maintains the computing resources for the user (customer) according to the requirements of the user. Security for the customers is key in a Public Cloud since the Cloud infrastructure is provided to several customers from the provider.

Private Clouds

Private Cloud environment is owned by the user company. The infrastructure – hardware, software or anything else -- is owned by the organization. The company manages all the computing resources needed for the functioning of the Cloud. Since the Cloud is entirely controlled by the company itself, the security risks associated with the Public Cloud are minimized in Private Clouds. However, the cost of maintaining and expanding the Private

Cloud are significantly higher than a Public Cloud since the company would need to invest in more hardware in order to expand the scale of the Private Cloud.

Hybrid Clouds

Hybrid Cloud environment uses the combination of private and public Clouds. In a Hybrid Cloud, a company's critical and sensitive information/data could be handled by the Private Cloud whereas relatively less critical data handling could be outsourced to the Public Cloud. Designing, managing and maintaining a Hybrid Cloud be a challenge due to the complexity of the mix the Cloud exists in.

Difference between these Cloud models

Type of Cloud	Ownership & Maintenance	Design & Scope	Example
Public	Owned and maintained by the Cloud Provider	Computing Resources (Hardware, Software and else) in the Cloud leased to multiple customers based on the SLA (Service Level Agreement). Cloud is available to multiple customers from the provider and security is key for each customer.	Amazon Cloud Services
Private	Owned and maintained by the company	Computing Resources (Hardware, Software and else) are private to the company and not available publically Cloud is private to the company and there are fewer security risks compared to Public Cloud.	Any company with their Private Cloud (IBM)
Hybrid	Owned partially by the Cloud Provider (Public Cloud) & the company (Private Cloud)	Computing resources (Hardware, Software and else) are shared based on the architecture design of the Hybrid Cloud	IBM

Cloud Models

Figure 1.4 shows a classic overview of Cloud models. Three types of models have been explained in the figure:

- Infrastructure as a Service (IaaS)

- Platform as a Service (PaaS)

- Software as a Service (SaaS)

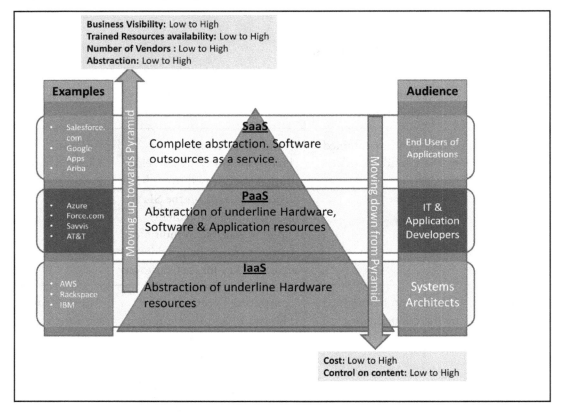

Figure 1.4

Infrastructure-as-a-Service (IaaS)

In the IaaS model, a Cloud Provider gives the infrastructure components -- hardware, software, networking, storage and other resources -- for a Cloud Customer based on a contract. The resources may not be pre-configured, hence placing the responsibility on the Cloud Customer to configure and manage the Cloud. These resources will be charged by the Cloud Provider based on the contract with the customer on the pay-per-use basis. A key resource in IaaS environment is a virtual server which is leased to the customer based on the processor capacity, storage requirement and memory needed.

Platform-as-a-Service (PaaS)

In the PaaS model, a customer is provided with a Cloud-based environment which is pre-deployed and configured, ready to be used by the customer. This Cloud environment can then be used to deliver the custom applications. The advantage of using PaaS is that the customer does not need to worry about the designing, configuring and maintaining the base Infrastructure needed for the application development. PaaS products include various software development environments which could be Java based for App Development.

Software-as-a-Service (SaaS)

In the SaaS model, the software runs from the Cloud which may be owned by a third party. The software could be available to users on a thin client via a web browser. SaaS enables the reusability of the software program to Cloud users, where the SaaS products are leased for various purposes using a Service Level Agreement. The user may have limited control over the SaaS implementation.

Difference between these Cloud models

Cloud Model	Feature	Granularity of Control for Customer	Customer Activities	Cloud Provider responsibility
IaaS	Virtualized IT resource and relative access to physical resources for the customer	Full access to all content, with full hardware control	Setting up the infrastructure, installing software and developing on top	Provisioning the physical server, storage, networking and other infrastructure required for the Cloud Customer

PaaS	Pre-configured platform available ready to use for customer. Limited or no control over the underlying infrastructure	Limited access to content and hardware	Using the platform to develop and deploy Cloud based solution	Preparation of the underlying IT infrastructure (hardware) and making the platform ready to use for the customer
SaaS	Access to software program in the Cloud	Configuration level access for making applications	Uses Cloud Service for an application	Managing, maintaining and monitoring Cloud Service

Cloud & OpenStack

OpenStack is a Cloud operating system which can tie together all IT resources and can provide that infrastructure to above layers. OpenStack can be used to deploy private, public or hybrid Cloud. It does come with all the characteristics of Cloud explained in this chapter.

OpenStack is basically an IaaS tool. The main task of OpenStack is to provision VMs and related services based on the above layers' requirements and automation. With every new release, more and more automation is coming in OpenStack and that is making it the choice of Cloud operating system.

Since it is open standard, almost most of the IT vendors are supporting OpenStack and hence there is no single vendor lock-in.

This book is dedicated to the internals of OpenStack. The following chapters will go through each module of OpenStack, and will have use cases if needed.

Chapter -2 | OpenStack

OpenStack

As per openstack.org –

"OpenStack is a Cloud operating system that controls large pools of compute, storage, and networking resources throughout a data center, all managed through a dashboard that gives administrators control while empowering their users to provision resources through a web interface"

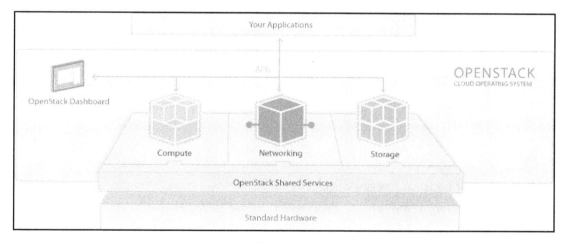

Figure 2.1
OpenStack overview – from OpenStack.org

As explained in figure 2.1, OpenStack is a Cloud operating system, which is abstracting the hardware from the applications. In Cloud context, the Cloud operating system is basically an IaaS (infrastructure as a service) operating system.

OpenStack is collaboration among developers around the globe who are working on forming an open source stack (Operating System) for Cloud infrastructure. The idea of OpenStack is to use the existing hardware and tools in data centers and come up with an open software which can be used as a free Iaas (Infrastructure as a service) operating system. To make it more robust and usable – the main aim is to make sure that OpenStack is able to manage huge data centers -- and achieve this level of scalability, the OpenStack is modular in nature and each component is designed to scale in its own context. When all the scaled components are put together, a highly scaled IaaS Cloud OS emerges, which is OpenStack.

In figure 2.1, it is also clear that OpenStack provides two types of handles for upper layers /software to access OpenStack (or its components). One way is directly accessing it via OpenStack dashboard (Horizon), another way would be to expose APIs to upper layer applications. In both cases, a good amount of automation can be done to do on-demand provision, etc.

History of OpenStack

OpenStack project started in July 2010 when NASA and RackSpace jointly launched an open source based Cloud platform (i.e., OpenStack). The major contributor at that point was NASA (by giving NOVA component) and Rackspace (by giving Swift). In later years, many companies started fueling this effort by contributing in this open source and making more applications (north bound and south bound) integrated with OpenStack.

The first release of OpenStack came in the winter of 2010, named Austin. This was more of proof of concept level of release. After this release there were many more releases that came after every few months. Every next release is better in features and simpler in implementation. Table 2.1 lists all the releases of OpenStack made so far.

Release Name	Release Month	OpenStack Components
Austin	October'10	Nova, Swift
Bexar	February'11	Nova, Swift, Glance
Cactus	April'11	Nova, Swift, Glance
Diablo	September'11	Nova, Swift, Glance

Essex	April'12	Nova, Swift, Glance, Horizon, Keystone
Folsom	September'12	Nova, Swift, Glance, Horizon, Keystone, Quantum, Cinder, Oslo
Grizzly	April'13	Nova, Swift, Glance, Horizon, Keystone, Quantum, Cinder, Oslo
Havana	October'13	Nova, Swift, Glance, Horizon, Keystone, Quantum, Cinder, Oslo, Heat, Ceilometer
IceHouse	April'14	

Table 2.1
Table explaining the releases of OpenStack

The naming convention follows the alphabetic order. One more thing to notice here is that with every new release, more components are getting added – increasing the usability and deployments. The release cycle is typically 6 months and rides with Ubuntu release cycle.

Why OpenStack

The story of OpenStack is exciting as a Cloud operating system, but general questions which can come to any new reader's mind are: –

• Why OpenStack?

• What is OpenStack trying to fix that was not working well earlier?

The customers (corporations, service providers, small and big business, researchers and global data centers) are looking to deploy large-scale Cloud deployments. To do this large scale deployment, the customers need a solid operating system which can tie the things together and can do automation for on-demand usage of these huge data centers. There are some solutions which available in the market, but those solutions come with known issues such as customer lock-in, incorrect pricing model, etc. Part of the problem is that with these huge data centers, having a single vendor IaaS OS may not even fly well.

OpenStack is trying to solve the same problem which has been solved by different vendors, but the approach is totally different and that's where OpenStack has got all the needed support and contribution from the development and customer community.

The OpenStack approach is to have Cloud OS as open, which prevents single vendor lock-in scenario, and also since it is open is highly cost-effective for all customers. As there are many companies contributing, the dependency on a single type of hardware will be very low, and hence it comes with the assurance that the solution will work with any hardware – which is the key to OpenStack success.

Characteristics of OpenStack

Figure 2.2 gives a basic definition of OpenStack, explaining where it fits in the triangle of the data center. The hardware is abstracted to the software layer and OpenStack sits in the middle of application and the huge data center resources.

- The hardware layer in the bottom is the biggest in any data center with a variety of appliances, routers, switches, servers, etc. It could be coming from many vendors and may have different usages for different types of functions.

- The application layer on the top is the layer which is a pure software driven layer, where the end-user makes (or runs) applications to use the massive hardware kept in data centers. Typically these applications are on-demand in nature and can have spikes / low time in their lifecycle.

- The middle layer is OpenStack, which essentially provisions the VMs on-demand, networks on-demand and storages on-demand. The provision is purely logical and a software applications (or customers) need not to know where the particular hardware is sitting which is hosting the data.

The two arrows depict that as we move towards application, the software defined nature of the stack becomes prominent and more automation can be introduced at that layer. However, towards the bottom of the pyramid it's more hardware focused and automation is more difficult to attain.

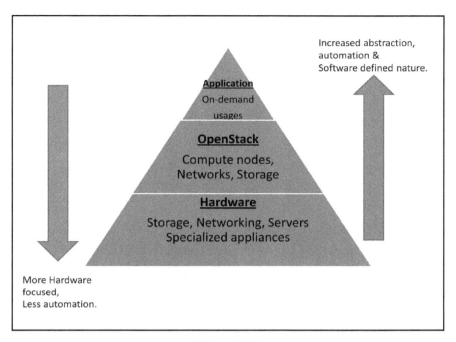

Figure 2.2
OpenStack in data centers

To get an overview of OpenStack, it is best to enumerate the characteristics of OpenStack, which are the key differentiators of OpenStack as compared to any Cloud OS.

- Collection of open source technology projects that provides an operating platform for orchestrating Clouds in a massive scale, thus keeping it simple to manage. Provide simple and scalable method of

  * Making VMs on-demand and snapshotting them in an easy way.

  * Attaching storage volumes to VMs on demand.

  * Making networks on demand

  * Provisioning object storage for VM images and arbitrary files

  * Provisioning multi-tenancy

- Have modular approach to the Cloud OS, while keeping the stack open source and provide easy integration between those modules. For the modularity, each and every module of OpenStack has minimum functional dependency on each other and for communication the standardized communication link is REST APIs (in some case it uses Rabbit MQ). Having the standard communication protocol and minimum dependency on inter-module working makes it easy to expand functionality at any time.

- Having a mechanism of making a platform independent OS which can run on any vendor's hardware and on other open technologies. OpenStack's key focus is to abstract the hardware from the software application running. To do that, it is needed that applications can be run on any type of hardware and there is minimal to no modification required in application code. To achieve this functionality OpenStack came up with Plugin approach for all vendors. The basic idea is to have a plugin in between the vendor hardware/software and OpenStack. The plugin will speak OpenStack language on OpenStack side and will translate those commands to native hardware language. Examples for that are Neutron Plugin, and Plugins for Storage, etc.

- Provide unified APIs to expose seamless integration with software applications. Each module of OpenStack communicates with external modules and applications using standard RESTfull APIs.

- Provide different method of Cloud provisioning – private, public, hybrid. The design and architecture is supposed to be such that it can support all Cloud deployment models.

- Providing the infrastructure which is elastic based on the demand. The basic idea is to have on-demand usage of the huge data center. OpenStack is fully elastic in provisioning VMs (the need would be generated by applications running on top of OpenStack). With Havana, the functionality auto-scaling came in, which is essentially template based service and template is deployed when it's needed.

- Provide method and simple way for metering and monitoring the usage of Cloud infrastructure. In the Havana release, the module named Ceilometer is fully capable of metering the system at different modules – compute nodes, network usage, etc.

- Provide a feature rich open platform for scaling Cloud. OpenStack is fully open and the code can be downloaded from its website. There are hundreds of developers in the OpenStack community working to make it feature-rich and ensure that it remains open.

- Low cost to maintain. With releases coming every ~6 months with bug fixes and new features, it's an easy OS to maintain. The user applications need not be impacted hugely with every release, because the communication protocol between OpenStack and user applications will not change – as that will remain as REST APIs.

- No specific vendor lock-in. OpenStack provides mechanism to make the hardware abstracted from the applications. This is the best advantage that OpenStack gives.

Components of OpenStack

OpenStack as a Cloud operating system is buildup of many modules. Each module provides a specific service to the OpenStack operating system. Figure 2.3 gives a snapshot of all those services:

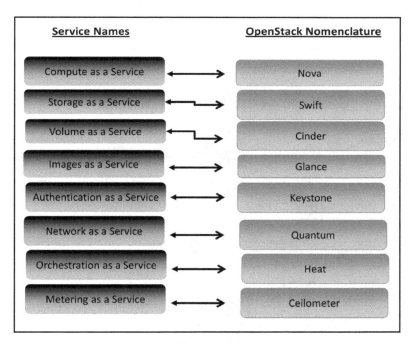

Figure 2.3
Modules of OpenStack

This book is divided on the basis of these modules and there is a chapter dedicated to each of these services, which goes into the details of these services.

OpenStack – A data center view

This book is all about explaining figure 2.4 in conceptual details. The portion of SDN and SDS is outside the scope of this book. In this figure, it is visible that OpenStack is truly a Cloud operating system and that it ties the hardware together to give a huge data center operating system which is modular and still does the same task.

The key thing to be looked at is that the whole hardware layer can be built on commodity hardware, which can be controlled by vendor plugins.

The top-most layer is software application layer, which is the layer where applications are written to provision the VMs and other resources of data center. Automation can be done on this layer by using simple REST API calls, and writing the business logic to call those APIs.

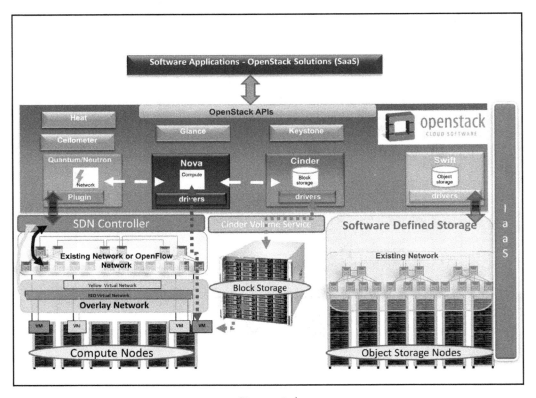

Figure 2.4
OpenStack Use Case

RESTfull APIs

OpenStack architecture is made up of modules which are mostly independent and they communicate with each other (or to the external world) using REST APIs. In the forthcoming chapters, this term will be used multiple times. So what is REST APIs?

REST stands for Representational State Transfer. It basically uses HTTP commands to execute any operation in OpenStack. These four commands are:-

- GET

- POST

- PUT

- DELETE

The API part of REST APIs is basically the APIs which can be called by these four commands. Using REST commands to invoke APIs is simple, scalable and standard. Many web services are adapting REST based communication by making APIs communicate using REST commands.

OpenStack - Why Open Matters?

All the code for OpenStack is freely available under the Apache 2.0 license. Any customer can download it for free and the best thing is that every 6 months or so, an upgrade is available. Because there are many vendors contributing in OpenStack space, the chances are that the customer will get the best solution. Having an open standard and software removes the fear of proprietary single vendor lock-in for customers, and create a large ecosystem that spans and scales.

Historically, the Open Standards always scaled better and became the success stories going forward. Here is the snapshot (figure 2.5) from trends.google.com, which compares OpenStack with some other Cloud operating systems in market. The spike in interest can be clearly seen in that.

In Figure 2.6, I have added AWS in the same comparison. It is clearly visible that AWS is far ahead than OpenStack. But the graphs are moving in the right direction and with open standards, OpenStack can potentially become the best choice for operating system of Clouds.

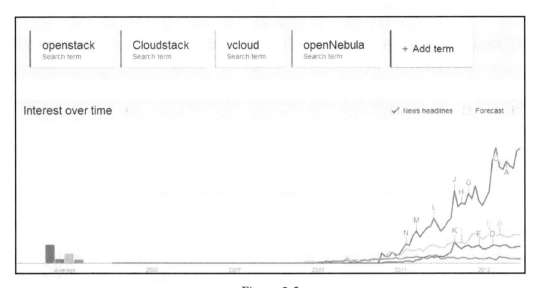

Figure 2.5
OpenStack trend compared to other Cloud Operating Systems

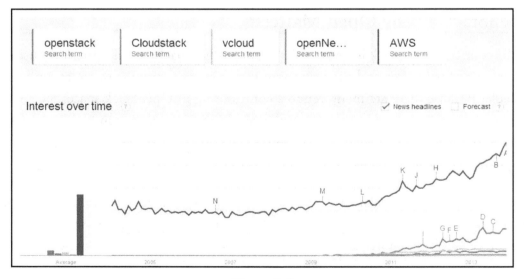

Figure 2.6
OpenStack trend compared to other Cloud Operating Systems (including AWS)

Chapter -3 | Keystone – Authentication as a Service

Authentication as a Service

For any user interactive system to work, an extensive framework of security system is needed. In typical systems a user is asked for the credentials and the credentials are matched with the real values (pre-shared or dynamically generated) and authentication, authorization and accounting is done.

In a complex system like OpenStack, where there is a multidimensional need for a security system, a dedicated component is needed which can take care of all security needs. The module was developed for the same and is named as Keystone. Keystone is supposed to have all information about users and their capabilities in multi service dimensions; it is also supposed to have a list of OpenStack services running in system – as the services need to contact Keystone for security.

Keystone, thus, is a service which provides authentication checking functionality when called for.

Overview of Keystone

Keystone is an OpenStack module that provides identity, token, catalog and policy services. Keystone is a one-stop shop for authentication service in OpenStack environment. All the operations (inter-module communication) typically get the authentication token from Keystone before it processes the requests coming from the other module.

Keystone can be described in the following way:

- Keystone is a framework to provide authentication as a service to all OpenStack users and other OpenStack services.

- Keystone does the request and response in JSON - RESTfull APIs.

- Keystone provides Policy, Token, Identity and Catalog services.

- Keystone provides service to authorize user for being part of different tenants and doing certain set of actions.

Variable Definition

Following are the variables which are needed in identification services.

Variable	Details
User	A person, system or an another service in OpenStack
Tenant	A group of similar characteristics users or resources
Token	A security clearance receipt which tells - what is accessible, how much, when & where.
Credentials	A set of user name / password, or something which represent the user uniquely.
Role	The role is defined based on the token or privilege given to a user.
Rule	A set of requirements to perform an action

Table 3.1
Keystone – Variable definition

Architecture of Keystone

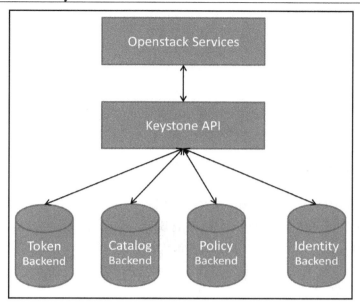

Figure 3.1
Architecture of Keystone

Token Backend

The token service does the AAA (authenticate, authorize and accounting) for the tokens used by different requests sent by tenant/user. This backend (Token backend) keeps and generates the information which is needed to run the Token service. The token backend could be based on KVS or memcache backend.

Catalog Backend

The catalog service provides endpoints information and this backend helps to kep track of all those endpoints. The catalogue backend can be based on SQL based of KVS based.

Policy Backend

This backend helps in providing all information related to authorization for users/tenants/roles, etc. It keeps all policies defined to authorize users, and is needed for policy service provided by Keystone. The backend used here is mainly a set of rules which are defined for users/tenants.

Identity Backend

This backend helps in providing all information related to credentials of users/tenants/roles, etc. It also has any meta-data which is needed to provide the identity service. The backend used here could be SQL based, KVS based or PAM based.

Keystone Communication with other Services

Keystone communicates using both JSON and XML data formats. The request is sent in the content –type header, and replies are sent back in accept header or sometimes in the body. The default communication is in JSON.

Keystone in Action

The following image is an example on how Keystone will provide "authentication as a service" to other services of OpenStack. Note that this example has taken some of the use cases; not all modules are covered in this example.

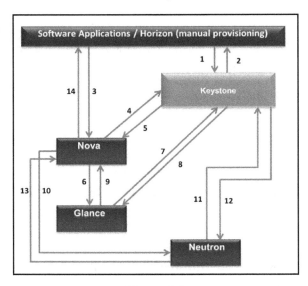

Figure 3.2
Keystone – In Action

Keystone - Authentication as a service for User

Step-1

Horizon sends HTTP request to Keystone for authentication with credentials. The credentials are in HTTP headers. The Keystone does following when it gets the HTTP request -

- The authentication is done on given credential.

- User-Tenant-Role mapping is validated.

- Decision on what all is user authorized for.

Step-2

Keystone sends temporary token to Horizon via HTTP.

Step-3

Horizon sends the POST request to Nova to start provisioning the VM, and gives the token information to validate the request.

Keystone - Authentication as a service for Compute

Step-4

Before moving to provision VM, Nova sends the token information to Keystone to verify if it's the valid token.

Step-5

Keystone validates the token and accepts or rejects it.

Step-6

Once Nova validates the token, it sends the information to Glance to provide the image with the token information to validate the request.

Keystone - Authentication as a Service for Image

Step-7

Before providing the image, Glance sends the token information to Keystone to verify if it's the valid token.

Step-8

Keystone validates the token and accepts or rejects it.

Step-9

Glance provides all information to Nova related to image.

Step-10

Nova sends the request for networks to Neutron along with the token information to validate the request.

Keystone - Authentication as a Service for Networks

Step-11

Neutron, before providing the network as a service, sends the token information to Keystone to verify if it's the valid token.

Step-12

Keystone validates the token and accepts or rejects it.

Step-13

Neutron provides all information that is Nova related to Networks.

Step-14

Finally, Nova reports to Horizon if the request is successful or not.

Chapter -4 | Nova – Compute as a Service

Compute as a Service

This is the most important service which OpenStack provides. For any data center, the bottom line is to measure how much computation power or how much storage it can support and then use that computation power by provisioning compute nodes. OpenStack provides computation as a service, which essentially means that it will be on-demand in nature and will be easily managed and provided as a service. This service uses underline hardware, which become totally abstracted for the software applications running on top of OpenStack.

Nova is the name of the module of OpenStack which provides the mechanism of compute as a service.

What is Nova

Nova is the name of the module which is used as a platform for OpenStack Cloud operating system. Typically Nova is the main component which is used to provision a VM. This is most complex module among many OpenStack modules.

Just like other OpenStack modules, Nova is not an independent module. Nova is a platform for OpenStack platform and the main controller of OpenStack is made up of Nova platform. However, the compute node portion of Nova runs on compute nodes. This compute node Nova works with Nova controller (the OpenStack controller).

The critical tasks of Nova can be listed as follows:

- Provisioning (starting, redefining, stopping and polling) virtual machines/instances.

- Adding/Editing/Deleting public IP addresses

- Adding/Editing/Deleting block storage

- Adding/Editing/Deleting security groups

Characteristics of Nova

Nova is the most important piece of OpenStack, and it has the following characteristics in its design:

- Nova comes with component based architecture. Nova is modular and is open to expansion and change as it evolves. To provide this architecture, Nova has many components attached to it, which are explained in detailed in this section.

- Nova comes with HA (high availability) feature. Nova provides an infrastructure which can support a highly scalable compute environment. Scalability comes with a need of HA.

- Nova comes with Fault-Tolerance functionality. As per the basic character of OpenStack, Nova is modular enough so that the faults from one module do not spread from one module to another.

- Nova is highly recoverable. Nova's recovery from faults is easy and it provides easy debugging ability.

Components of Nova

Nova is a collection of several features and components, which enables Nova to satisfy all the characteristics mentioned above. As Nova components communicate to each other using messaging queues, etc.,, there is no need to have all the components on one server. These components can be installed on one machine (server) or on different servers. Here are the details of components of Nova compute:

Nova Component	Details
Nova-API	Main task is to accept and work on the API calls from OpenStack Horizon or Amazon EC2.

Nova-scheduler	It looks into the existing load and decides on which host the new VM should be homed.
Nova-DB	SQL based database which keeps the information of all VMs provisioned in the system.
Nova-conductor	Helps in communication between Nova-compute and Nova-DB. Nova-compute cannot access Nova-DB directly.
Nova-compute	Nova-compute is the one responsible for provisioning VM working with Hypervisors and getting initiations signals from Nova-API for provisioning and deletion of VMs.
Nova-queue	Nova-queue is responsible for passing messages between different Nova components and other OpenStack components. It is implemented in Rabbit queue mainly.

Table 4.1
Nova Components

Where do all these components stay in OpenStack environment:

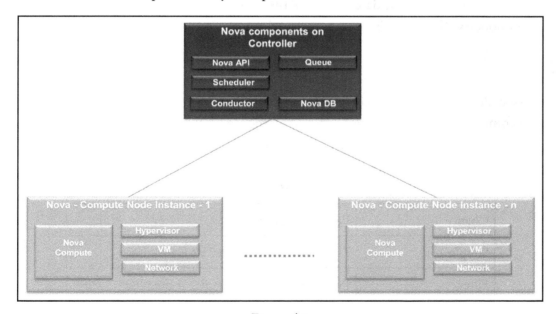

Figure 4.1
Nova Components

As figure 4.1 explains, some components stay on the OpenStack controller and some stay on Compute noted instance. In a typical deployment, compute nodes are separate from controller node, but having compute node of controller node can also work. However, in either case, the communication between different components will happen via Nova queue.

There can be more controllers for bigger OpenStack deployments; more controllers can share the load between all controllers in deployments. Below are the details for these components.

Nova-API

At the heart of the OpenStack Cloud framework is the Nova API Service (Ken Pepple). Nova-API is a RestFull HTTP based service which is used to interact within Nova and with other components of OpenStack. The API endpoints are basic HTTP web services which talk to Keystone for security tokens, talks to Horizon/Amazon EC2 for getting provision information and talk to other components of OpenStack for provisioning VMs.

By default, Nova-API listens on port 8774 for the OpenStack API. To accept and fulfill API requests, Nova-API initiates most of the provisioning activities, and also enforces security policies. Nova-API is a HA ready service.

Nova-scheduler

Nova-scheduler is a daemon which runs on controller and it's main job is to decide that which compute node in the OpenStack system should provision a new VM. Following are some types of scheduling algorithms which Nova-scheduler supports.

Type of Scheduler	Behavior of the Scheduler
Chance	Pick a random host
Simple	Pick a host that has least VMs running
Filter	Pick a host that is a best fit for the filter

Table 4.2

Scheduler in action

All compute nodes periodically publish their status, resources available and hardware capabilities to Nova-scheduler through the queue and Nova database. Nova-scheduler then collects this data from the database and uses it to make decisions when a request comes in.

In figure 4.2, an example of OpenStack system with 6 Compute nodes is explained. The example is taken for 6 compute nodes available to provision the VM. Table 4.3 shows the details of those 6 compute nodes current status (CNs):

Compute Node	RAM value (GB)	Number of current instances running
CN -1	32	3
CN -2	16	2
CN -3	32	1
CN -4	32	0
CN -5	16	0
CN -6	32	5

Table 4.3

Based on the table, we can see the snapshot of a running system indicating which CN (compute node) has how much RAM and how many VMs are working on what.

With this state, let's say a scheduling filter says that the VM should be hosted on any CN which has more than 24 GB of RAM. Then the scheduling will happen as mentioned in figure 4.2:

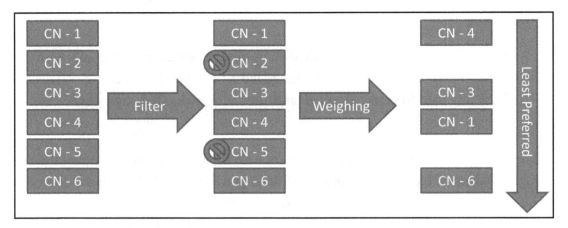

Figure 4.2
Nova-scheduler in action

Based on the filter definition, CN-2 and CN-5 will be out of the selection process. Nova scheduling on crossing the filters will look at the weight and cost of the remaining machines and will assign one of the CNs to host the VM. In this example, the weight and cost is based upon the "simple" algorithm that whichever CN has fewest VMs running will host the new VM, also the filter is taken as an example of RAM. There may be other algorithms to calculate weight, costs and filters.

Nova-db

Nova-db is the relational database which stores the information related to OpenStack variables. Mainly, it will include the following information:

- Run time state of Virtual Machines.

- Volume information for block storage.

- Credential / token information.

- Key information.

- Network information.

Nova-db is backbone of Nova when it comes to having the information for all run variables. The events when Nova-db is accessed during the operation of OpenStack VM provisioning are the following:

- Interacts with Nova-scheduler for providing the compute nodes information, so the scheduler can decide on which node the VM should be hosted.

- Interacts with Nova-compute (compute nodes), via Nova-conductor to provide the information for instance ID, etc,, and also to update its database about the compute node.

Nova-conductor

Nova-conductor is a service which is available from OpenStack Grizzly release. The main job of this service is to save (abstract) Nova-db from direct access. It sits in-between nova-db and other services, and acts as a bridge between them. The way it is implemented is explained in figure 4.3.

Characteristics of Nova-conductor

- Provides security to Nova-db by restricting direct access by any other service.

- Provides a way to horizontal scaling; as it is a service so many instances can be made.

- It abstracts the database complexities from outer services, which makes it easy to have any db implemented (as long as conductor understands it)

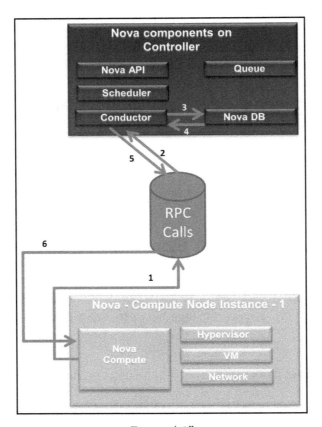

Figure 4.3"
Nova-cConductor

Figure 4.3 explains the events which happen at the time when Nova-compute node tries to read the Nova-db while provisioning a VM on it.

Step-1: When Nova-compute gets a signal to provision a VM on its instance it sends a RPC call.

Step-2: The RPC call is sent to conductor.

Step-3: The conductor converts the calls to database query and reads/write the data base. The conductor will understand on what kind of database it is talking to. (Note that Nova-compute need not know what kind of database Nova-db has).

Step-4: The Nova-db returns the value to conductor.

Step-5: The Nova-conductor sends the information via RPC call.

Step-6: The RPC call returns the data to Nova-compute.

Nova-queue

Nova-queue is a communication link between different components of Nova. Nova-queue is based on AMQP(Advanced Message Queue Protocol). AMQP can be implemented in Rabbit-MQ or Qpid. Nova-queue is the communication link between following nova components:

- Nova-API

- Nova-conductor

- Nova-compute

- Nova-scheduler

Communication types for Nova-queue

OpenStack uses RPC calls to communicate between different components of Nova. RabbitMQ supports the following communications

- RPC calls: Having an asynchronous communication which is based on request and response , with a call back when there is a reply for a request.

- RPF cast: These are just one time messaging events, without waiting for a response.

Nova-queue benefits

- Making the nova nodes truly component based. By having the RabbitMQ queue, the two components will not need to know the state of other components before starting communication.

- Since it is queue based architecture, it is a balanced way of having communication between all components of Nova.

Nova-compute

Nova-compute is a daemon which creates or deletes VM using hypervisor API. Compute node by itself is just a machine running with a hypervisor. Nova compute works with that hypervisor and does the needed virtualization by provisioning VMs and related services with it.

Nova-compute controls how many tenants, projects, etc., can be launched on a particular compute node. Working with Nova controller in the scheduling process, it helps making the system reliable. Nova-compute helps giving that information in scheduling process. Nova comes up with this information by looking at mainly the following:

- CPU cores and usage of the compute node

- Total RAM and its usage of the compute node

- Remaining Floating IPs or Fixed IPs

As explained in figure 4.4, during the provisioning operation of the VM, Nova-compute acts as glue between compute node and other modules of OpenStack. The main task which is undertaken by Nova-compute daemon is working with:

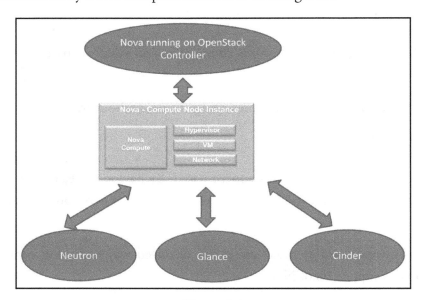

Figure 4.4

- Cinder and local hypervisor to attach a volume

- Work with Glance to get the image to boot the VM.

- Work with Neutron to attach the IP address to the VM

This interaction is needed when VM is provisioned and also at the time of deleting it (Nova does not talk to Glance while deleting the VM).

Chapter -5 | Glance – Image as a Service

Image as a Service

Image as a service, as suggested, is a concept for having on-demand VM image, as and when there is need to provision an image. While providing the Image as a service following are the key characteristics that need to be taken care to support requests coming in:–

- Have a catalogue of all available images, which is searchable for consumers.

- Have real images stored in attached devices.

- Have generic APIs, so any service can ask for the image using simple language.

- Support, store and provide any kind of image abstracting the storage and other internal details.

- Highly available for other components.

In OpenStack, the module which provides the Image as a service is known as Glance. This chapter is dedicated to explain Glance in details.

Overview of Glance

Glance - Image as a Service provides search, registration, and fetch and delivery services for VM images. Glance can have the images saved as template and can get new server up and running quick. Glance hides the complexity of how the image is saved, so the image requesting components are abstracted from the type of storage which is used for the image storage. Glance provides a standard REST APIs for interfacing between it and other component.

Like Nova, Glance also communicates internally with its components to provide an end-to-end service. Glance listens on port number 9292.

Glance can - Create, Read, Update, Delete images. This is typically known as CRUD images. Glance can Search images via filters

- Name of the image

- Format of the container which is having image

- Format of the disk which is holding the image

- Size of the image

Glance also Caches the images, so it can be faster on replies.

- It mainly uses SQLite for caching

- It makes a queue of images which are candidates for caching.

- It prunes and cleans the images which are no longer needed.

Glance - Supported image formats

Glance supports following image types as of now in Grizzly release –

Image Format	Details
raw	Unstructured disk image format.
qcow2	A disk format supported by the QEMU emulator that can expand dynamically and supports copy-on-write.
vhd	VHD disk format, a common disk format used by virtual machine monitors from VMWare, Xen, Microsoft, VirtualBox, and others.
vmdk	Disk format is used by the compute service's VMware API.
iso	An archive format typically used for the data contents of an optical disc (e.g., CDROM, DVD).
vdi	A disk format supported by VirtualBox virtual machine monitor and the QEMU emulator

aki	An Amazon kernel image.
ari	An Amazon ramdisk image.
ami	An Amazon machine image.

Table 5.1
Glance – Supported images

Glance components

Glance has three components which make it functional for image as a service in OpenStack. Figure 5.1 explains different components of Glance.

The main components are:

- Glance API

- Glance Catalogue (registry)

- Glance Database

- Data Store (not part of Glance, but may be needed in some cases).

Glance API

Glance API, like Nova API, is the interface of Glance with other services which uses Glance for Image as a Service. Once the request comes, it sends the requests to other Glance components. Internal components can be of any complexity, but the main job of Glance API is to hide all the complexities and give an open standardized way to communicate for Image services.

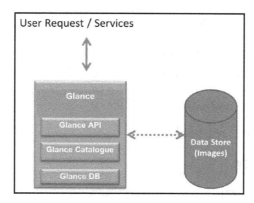

Figure 5.1
Glance components

Glance Catalogue (Registry)

Glance-registry should be up and running to support Glance API. Glance API uses glance registry for accessing the Glance database. There are some versions of OpenStack, wherein Glance-API can access the Glance-db directly, but the standard is to have the DB access via registry using REST API (JSON). Glance registry contains meta-data about the images and has it in the form of catalogue. Glance registry listens on port number 9191. Any web service which satisfya the Glance REST API standards can be used for Glance catalogue service.

Glance DB (database)

For storing the metadata for the images, Glance uses the database which runs on the same server where Glance-API is running. Glance uses SQLite by default. It may also be configured to use MySQL or PostgreSQL.

Data Store for Glance

Also known as Glance backend, it stores all the actual images to provide them when the service is needed. Following are the supported backends as Glance data store (backend) –

- Swift (OpenStack's object storage)

- Local file system (Default storage for Glance, to store the images on the local server).

- S3 (Glance can keep the images in Amazon's backend storages – S3).

- HTTP communication – Glance can communicate to any server via HTTP to get the image which is stored on it. For having this type of backend, the two conditions are –

  * The server should be reachable via HTTP.

  * This kind of storage is read only.

Glance Architecture

Figure 5.2 explains on how Glance communicates with in itself. As explained in the figure, once Glance-API gets request from the external components, the Glance-API will request the information from Glance Catalogue. The catalogue will have the information cached (in most of cases) and it will provide that meta-data to Glance-API; if the information is not cached, then it will pull the data from Glance-DB to give all information. When Glance-registry gives the data back to Glance-API (using REST APIs), it will also send the URL of the image on data store. The data store can be anything ranging from Swift to HTTP reachable via internet.

Once Glance-API has the information on image, it can serve the other components for OpenStack for providing image as a service.

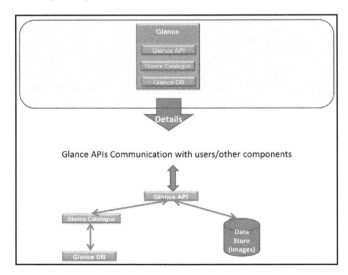

Figure 5.2
Glance Architecture

Chapter -6 | Cinder : Volume as a Service

Cinder - Volume as a Service (Block)

Cinder provides volumes to VMs provisioned by the OpenStack. It was segregated from Nova during Essex release. Like other components of OpenStack, it uses RESTfull APIs for communicating with different components. The volumes can be solid state drives, or regular drives. Also, the drives can be sitting in the same compute nodes where the VM is provisioned, or it can be a dedicated storage device which is connected to compute nodes via iSCSI or FC.

Characteristics of Cinder

- Provides persistence block storage for VMs

- Uses NFS, CIFS types of well-established file system.

- Provides a service where additional persistence storage can be added on the fly.

- The access can be restricted within a VM.

- On-demand usage.

- Need not be on the compute node, it can accessible via iSCSI or FC.

- Has typical OpenStack characteristics like:

  * High availability
  * Modularity
  * Open Standards
  * RESTfull APIs.

Components of Cinder

Figure 6.1 explains the basic components of Cinder and also how it fits the OpenStack environment. Following are the main components of Cinder:

• Cinder API

The Cinder API is a set of defined RESTfull APIs which can be accessed from OpenStack controller or by a user defined application. The basic job of this set of API is to get request and do the required action.

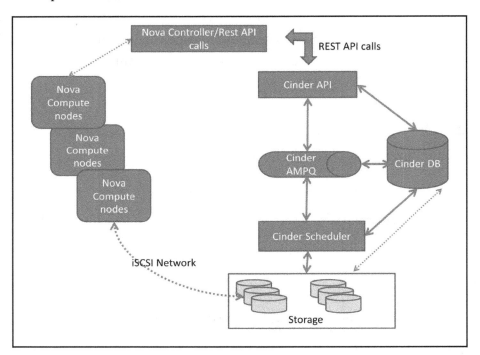

Figure 6.1
Overview of Cinder

• Cinder Database

Cinder database is a normal SQL based data base and it is accessible by each component of Cinder. It stores the details of which volume has been given to which VM. This database also serves as one of the input variables for Cinder scheduler.

- Cinder AMPQ

Cinder AMPQ is a rabbit MQ which is used as a message queue for communication between the components of Cinder. The details of Rabbit MQ are explained in Nova chapter. Cinder uses direct, fan-out, and topic-based messages in the queue.

- Cinder scheduler

Cinder scheduler takes the responsibility for assigning the volume based on the usage and demand.

- Block Storage

The backend storage which are used by Cinder are typically high end storage, as the purpose is to provide persistence data storage for VMs. However the data storage could be made up of solid state storage or typical hard drive with spindle.

- iSCSI Networks

As of now, the communication between block storage and Compute nodes (for which Cinder provides the volume service) happens via iSCSI.

Cinder Plugins

Cinder provides a mechanism to ensure that various vendors with different architecture are compatible with OpenStack architecture. This compatibility is accomplished by providing a vendor plugin option for different vendors. The concept is same as Neutron Plugin.

Chapter -7 | Swift: Block Storage as a Service

Storage as a Service (Object)

The way we share, keep and generate information has totally changed in the past few years. The data storage demands nowadays have totally different charters as compared to what it used to have a few years back. The data storage demand in current data centers have the following characteristics.

- The data needs are not synchronous with computation need. For example, companies like DropboxInc are much more data storage centric as compared to computation needs.

  * Think about Dropbox data center – it will need more storage as compared to computation power.

- The applications become more read/write intensive. For example, in companies like Facebook, thousands of pictures are accessed per minute.

  * Think about the Facebook data center – it will need more storage as well as a very effective way of doing I/O.

- The applications become global, so user base is sparser compared to what it used to be earlier. From storage point of view it boils down to have data replicated locally for local users, while having high availability.

  * Think about a Gmail user in India, will he/she have data stored in US or in Asia? And what happens if the Asian data center goes down?

- Demand of data storage in data centres is increasing exponentially. There is constant pressure on data centres to keep the cost increment linear, and finding ways to make sure that cost is not proportional to increased demand.

  * Commoditization of storage is needed, as it was done for servers few years back.

OpenStack being the operating system of data center fabric, has come up with the component named Swift which is dedicated to providing object storage in data centers. This module is not integrated with other components of OpenStack (except Keystone, and partly with Glance).

OpenStack Object Storage (Swift) is open source OpenStack Cloud computing project component, known as object storage, which provides powerful scalability, redundancy and durability.

This chapter is dedicated to Swift.

Overview of Swift

Swift was one of the base components which was developed in OpenStack. It was initially developed by Rackspace along with NASA. The following are the characteristics of the Swift module:

- Highly scalable

- Durability by 3 times of replications

- Supports RESTfulapis like other components of OpenStack

- Design based on putting commodity storage devices at work

- Supports distributed architecture

- Supports multi tenancy

- Supports high concurrency

- Open source based, to provide open standard.

How Swift works is explained in figure 7.1.

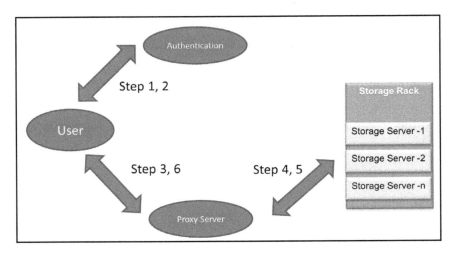

Figure 7.1
Overview of Swift

This figure is a very high level view of the swift operation. The User in this figure could be any REST API based request coming from middleware or from the OpenStack environment. Authentication server is Keystone, and proxy server is the proxy server of Swift.

On conceptual level, these are the steps taken to have Sswift working:

Step -1: User sends the authentication request to Authentication server.

Step-2: Server responds with the authentication token.

Step-3: User sends a Put or Get command to proxy server.

Step-4: Proxy server selects one of the storage nodes (based on algorithms), and does Put or Get operation.

Step-5: Proxy server replies to the user with the request (Put or Get)

Components & Concepts of Swift

Like any other module of OpenStack, Switch also is modular in nature and has the following high level components in switch module. Figure 7.1 gives the pictorial presentation of the components.

Proxy server

Swift proxy servers are the glue between all components of Swift. It exposes the APIs for external access, and gives the right path for object, container and account. In case of failure of a particular object, it will get the requests routed from ring.

The Ring

The Ring is responsible for deciding where the data will be stored in a cluster. It has the mapping between the physical data and the entity name given to it. There are three kinds of Rings:

- Account Ring

- Container Ring

- Objects Ring

Each type of Ring is the contact point for doing any operation on above three components.

The other, rather, main task of Ring is to make sure that physical data (which is measured in a unit of partition) is replicated three times in different zones/clusters. The Ring will have the information for these 3 locations and will use the information in case of failover. When new physical devices are added in the Swift system, the Ring adjusts itself to have more space, etc.

Note – Partition is a set chunk of storage space which stores Objects, Account DB, Container DB.

Accounts

Account is equivalent to a user in the Swift system. This is essentially a database which keeps tracks that how many containers are associated with a particular account.

Containers

Container is logical grouping of objects (the real data). An account will have the list of all containers, and each container will keep a list of all objects. This list of objects has no role in doing a look-up while reading data from object, but it's used to indexing it for accounting purposes.

Object Servers (or Objects)

In OpenStack environment, object is referred as real data. The Object servers are the real servers, which will store the data. These Object servers are further divided in terms of Zones, etc.

Zones

Zone is the logical partition of the storage drives. The data is typically stored in Zone basis and the replication happens in different Zones, so if one Zone fails the data can be fetched from another Zzone.

Replication

The main job of replicator is to make sure that data is replicated in different locations, the data does not get corrupted when it is copied and in case of data delete operation – it makes sure that data is deleted from all locations.

It uses the hash value comparison to make sure that data is consistent.

Updaters

When the data is not replicated immediately because of some reason – it's the updater's job to update the replication looking at the queue of objects which are not replicated.

Auditors

These are the programs which scan the databases and objects to make sure that data is not corrupted. If it finds that data is corrupted, the file will be replaced by replication and the corrupted files will be deleted.

Architecture of Swift

Figure 7.2 explains the overall Sswift in a single picture. The same diagram has logical and physical views shown together. All the components in Swift are shown indicating where they fall in place. A simple use case of upload of a file and download of a file is given.

During upload the request will come to put a file in storage. The load balancer will put that in one of the proxy servers. The proxy server will then look up that in which Zone the data is, and it will send the request to Object Ring to get the exact physical location of the Zone/Partition. The Object Ring will access the objects in that Zone. The Zone is shown to be made up of physical servers, and storage further has Partitions. So eventually the data will reside on one or more Partitions of those Zones.

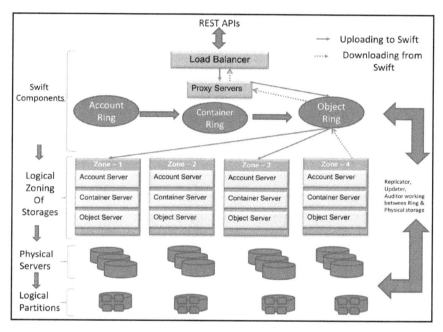

Figure 7.2
Swift Architecture

During download the request will come to get a file from storage. The load balancer will put the request in one of the proxy servers. The proxy server will then look up in which Zone the data is and it will send a get request to that Zone to Object ring. The Object Ring will look for the exact location and read the data and give it back to where the request came from.

One the right side of the diagram, a block is shown which explains on how Replicator, Updater and Auditor works in this whole system. They have the access to partitions and they access those to do the maintenance job, as explained in the component section of this chapter.

Chapter -8 | Neutron – Network as a Service

Neutron – Network as a Service

As other services in OpenStack, Neutron is responsible for providing networks for communicating between different VMs in an OpenStack system. When a VM comes up in an OpenStack environment, it needs an IP address to start communicating; Neutron does that job. Here are a few characteristics of Neutron:

- It provides API to make complex networking topologies, policies and setup communication between VMs.

- It is open to having plugins from different vendors, so the networks can be made on any vendor's networking devices.

- It provides a way for service insertion - like Firewall as a service, or load balancer as a service.

- It is integrated with Horizon to provide an easy way to configure networks (Make and Delete).

Components of Neutron – Networking as a Service:

As per the conceptual diagram of OpenStack, the following components are part of Neutron – Networking as a Service, in OpenStack context.

- Neutron Server

- Neutron plugin

- Neutron agent

- DHCP agent

- L3 agent

- Neutron database

All the above components run on controller, or on network node, or on compute node. In most cases, network node runs on the same machine as does the controller.

Neutron Server

The Network as a Service - Neutron server -- runs on the controller node of OpenStack or on the network node of the OpenStack cluster (it can run on separate node or on the same machine where controller is running), it exposes the OpenStack Networking API and passes user requests to the networking plugin for controlling the network devices. As per current designs most of the SDN controllers access the Neutron server databases using Neutron plugins.

Neutron plugin

The plugin is vendor specific software which runs on the network node (or controller); the plugin's job is to interact with neutron server and access the database. Note that not all vendors provide Neutron plugin along with Neutron agent – it depends on how vendors have implemented the plugin. It runs on the network node.

Note: In some cases, the vendor plugin overrides the DHCP and L3 plugins (which comes native with OpenStack).

Neutron agent

Neutron agent is vendor specific software (which works in tandem with Neutron plugin); It runs on the compute node hypervisor. This is a vendor specific plugin agent, which talks to Neutron server or to the Neutron plugin running on Neutron server.

DHCP agent

DHCP agent runs by default on the network node. The main task for DHCP plugin is to provide the IP address to the newly added VM. When a subnet is created, the DHCP for that subnet is automatically enabled.

L3 agent

Layer 3 (L3) agent runs on the network node. The main task for L3 agent is to provide layer 3 forwarding and also provide floating IPs when it's needed.

Other Concepts

Floating IPs

Every time a VM comes up it will need an IP address. This IP address could be a public IP address or a private IP address. As the name suggests, the difference between private IP and public IP is where they communicate. Private IP communicates between VM instances and public IP communicates with the outside world.

The IP address can be assigned in two ways: fixed or floating IP address. In a fixed IP address method, the VM will come up with a fixed IP address or with a floating IP address.

Floating IP address is a set of IP addresses decided by the Cloud administrator and it is assigned on a per project/tenant basis. The floating IP set depends upon the quota which is given to that project/tenant.

The benefit with Floating IP address is that when a VM comes up, the IP address can be associated automatically and can be de-associated when the VM goes down (or sometimes it can be de-associated when VM is up).

Networking Architecture of OpenStack

Figure 8.1 shows the high level design of networking components which have been explained in earlier chapters. On a very high level, there are three components of Networking:

- Network Node: This is the networking module which hosts the agents; this module can be installed on a separate machine or it can be installed on the same machine where OpenStack controller is running. It has the following agents running:

  * L3 Agent
  * DHCP agent

    * Vendor's plugin

- Neutron Server: This server keeps all networking related information in its database, etc. The main components in a Neutron Server are:

    * Database

    * Neutron Server

    * Vendor's Plugin

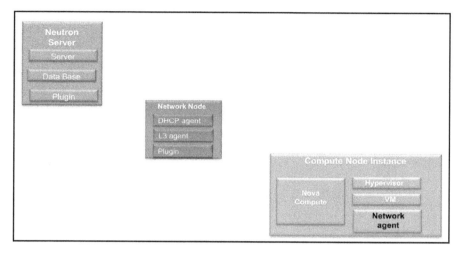

Figure 8.1
High Level Neutron

- Network agent on each compute node: This small piece runs on each compute node making sure that there is communication between compute nodes and other networking components. The main components are:

    * Physical NIC

    * OVS or Linux bridge

    * Vendor's Plugin

In this chapter, the focus is more on how Neutron works, and how the plugin works on Neutron Sserver, network node and on compute node.

The plugin implementation process can be different for different vendors. Some vendors use underlined OVS functionality and some vendors do not use that. How much plugin code runs on Neutron server and how much it runs on compute node (as a neutron agent) is also vendor specific. The example given below shows a Neutron working taking OVS as base plugin.

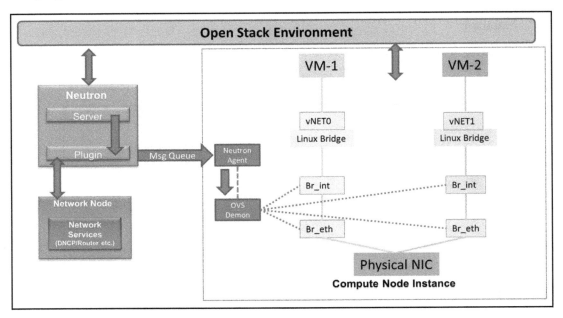

Figure 8.2
Details of Neutron working

In figure 8.2, a typical deployment with OVS plugin is explained. In the example, there are two VMs on compute node (VM-1 and VM-2), both the VMs are in different VLANs. The Network node block could be running on separate machine or on the controller itself). A controller is shown which is running on the server. The Neutron agent sits on the compute node, and talks to Neutron plugin running on network node. The Neutron plugin reads and write the Neutron database.

In compute node, a very high level description of internal components is shown. There are four types of virtual networking devices involved in compute node:

• TAP device

  * In the figure it is shown as vnet0. This is typically a vNIC which is created by the hypervisor when the VM is provisioned.

- Linux bridge

  * Linux bridge is basically a hub; any packet coming to one of the ports of it will go out on all ports.

- OVS bridge

  * OVS bridge is a virtual switch bridge; the VLANs can be assigned at this level – as you can do in regular physical switch.

- VETH Pairs

  * It's a simple one-to-one connection of two virtual devices; a packet sent from one end should reach the other end.

Note: In the figure, br_int and br_ext are part of OVS. br_int is the bridge integration module internally (like connecting to Linux bridge), br_ext is the module which connects to physical NIC.

As per OpenStack documentation, if the packet has to come out from VM's vnet and has to go out from physical NIC, it has to go through 9 points (these 9 points are made up of above 4 devices).

Operation details:

When a VM is provisioned, the Linux bridge and TAP devices take care of bringing up the vNIC for that particular VM. However, when the information of those VM reaches OVS bridge (the br_int and br_ext) ports, the OVS override the configurations by whatever is configured by Neutron plugin/agent. At this level, the VLANs, etc., can be defined and overridden. The neutron plugin keeps the check on VLAN and other networking parameters by keeping the entry in the database for each VM configurations. which VM has what configuration etc.

Use Cases for OpenStack Networking

This section explains the different scenarios which can be supported by OpenStack. Like traditional networking, these use cases are more of those based on segregated networks versus flat networks. As per OpenStack documentation, it recognizes the following use cases for networking:

- Single flat network

- Multiple flat networks

- Mixed flat and private network

- Provider router with private network

- Per tenant router with private networks

Each type of network is used for a specific deployment. As the need of deployment could be public, hybrid or private Cloud, these deployment models help as template design. The Neutron module of OpenStack has the capability to support these models.

Single flat network

As explained in figure 8.3 below, in this deployment it's a single VLAN deployment wherein any host can talk to any host and it's flat. All the VMs will have IPs from same subnet, and there will be a common gateway router for them.

These sets of IPs can be given via fixed IP method or can also be given using floating IP concept. This deployment is used when the deployment is small private Cloud, and there is no restriction of which VM can talk to which VM.

In the figure, all the machines (no matter which tenant it is hosting) come under a flat network of 10.0.0.0/8 flat network.

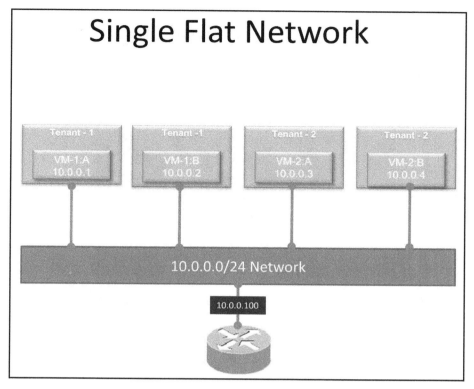

Figure 8.3
Single Flat Network

Multiple flat networks

As explained in figure 8.4, in this deployment it's a multiple VLAN deployment wherein any host in a single flat network can talk to any host in that network. All the VMs in one flat network will have IPs from same subnet, and there will be a common gateway router for each flat network. The same router can be used for the multiple flat networks – as long as they are in a separate subnet. The other fact which is shown in the figure is that a single tenant can host VMs from multiple flat networks.

This deployment gives the ability to create logical networks across multiple tenants.

In figure 8.4, the machine hosting tenant-3 is having two VMs coming from two different flat networks (10.0.0.0/8 & 10.0.1.0/24). Rest of the machine (no matter which tenant it belongs to) is part of just one flat network.

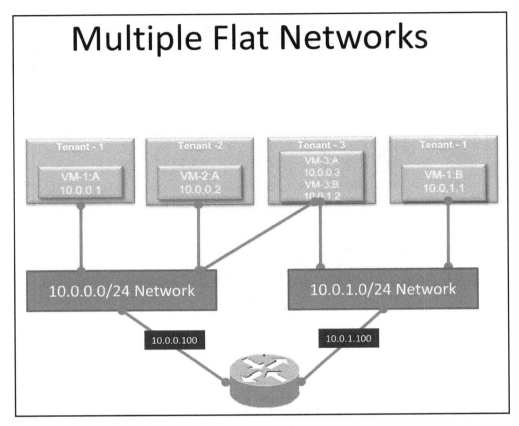

Figure 8.4
Multiple Flat Network

Mixed flat and private network

As the name suggests and is shown in figure 8.5, this is a mix of a flat network and a private network. The private network, as per its definition, is the network which is not exposed to the external network. As shown in the figure, the tenant can choose to have all private VMs and/or have VMs which are exposed to the external gateway. If the tenant has private VMs, by nature the traffic generated by those will not be shared outside the network, until there is no NAT service is provisioned.

This model shows the design of a multi-tier architecture.

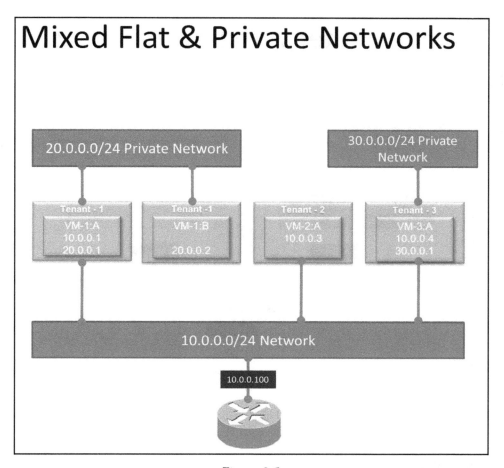

Figure 8.5
Multiple Flat& Private Network

External router with private network

This use case is explained in figure 8.6. This use case has tenants with their own private network and having external routing interface. As explained in figure 8.6, the machines hosting tenant-1 and 2, will be part of two networks, the first network 10.x is internal to tenants, and network 20.x is exposed for external routers.

Here the VMs on the tenants can be given IP addresses by floating IP addresses pools.

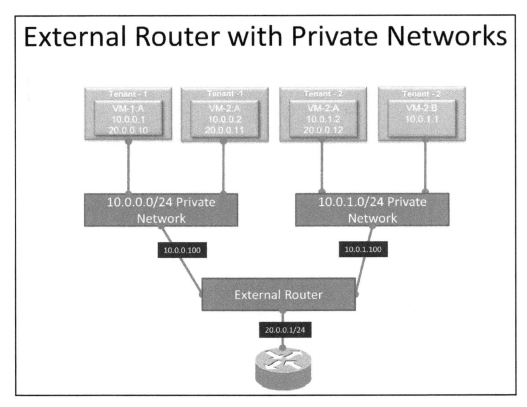

Figure 8.6
External Router with Private Network

Per tenant router with private networks

As explained in figure 8.7, this use case explains the scenario wherein each tenant will have its own private network and its own external router. This is different from figure 8.6 where there is a single external router.

The tenant can make his own private network and IP address can be allocated from the floating pool, and external uplink IPs can be given from floating pool or from manual configurations.

This design is again a multi-tier architecture for the tenants and routing on the uplink.

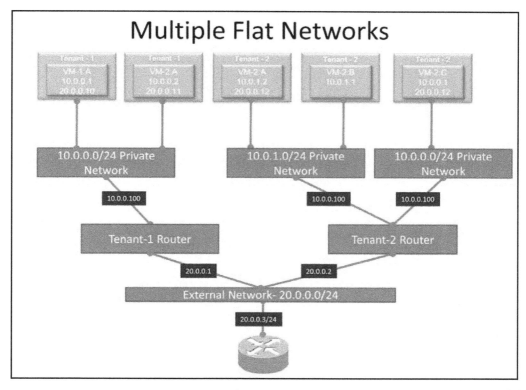

Figure 8.7
External Router with Private Network

Implementing Different Use Cases – How Neutron does it?

The use cases section above shows that there are many combinations on how VMs and tenants can be provisioned on compute node and also that there are multiple ways on how these VMs can talk to each other and to the external world.

The question is, how the compute node canbe configured with so many combinations, especially given the fact that the implementation inside compute host networking is just made up of Linux making vNIC and OVS giving VLAN information, etc. Shown below is the explanation of two different scenarios – how it works in a flat network vs a tagged network (if we put the IP address on these VMs in these cases, the same case gets translated into single subnet and multiple subnet examples).

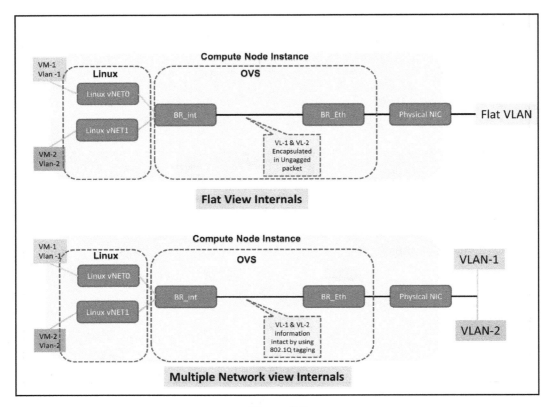

Figure 8.8
Neutron internal – Flat network vs multiple network

As explained in figure 8.8, the above section (Flat View Internals) is how the information is passed where there are two VM in same VLAN. The Linux bridge brings up the VM and then passes the information to br_int. As explained earlier, – br_int and br_eth is controlled by Neutron plugin/agent via OVS; now if it's a flat network then the packets coming from VM-1 and VM-2 go untagged and come out as VLANflat on the physical NIC.

However, as explained in the following section (Multiple Network view Internals), if there are two VLANs (each for a VM), then the OVS will tag those packets coming from br_int and going out of br_eth into respective VLANs, and physical NIC will have two different broadcast domains and packet will come out on two VLANs.

End-to-end View

This chapter goes into the details of how neutron works and how it interacts with hypervisors, etc. Earlier sections in this chapter have explained how a single compute node (hypervisor) handles a flat or a multiple network.

This section of the chapter is about how all this technology looks like in a typical deployment of switches/routers and Servers. Figure 8.9 gives an example of two compute nodes connected via multiple routers and switches (the network could be made up of OpenFlow).

The SDN controller depicts the controller which controls the networking devices in vendor native protocol and, on the other side, it communicates with OpenStack plugin. The deployment may come even without SDN controller, because the existing network need not have SDN capabilities, the existing networking protocols and equipment are usable in that case However there has to be some plugin from the networking vendors which can communicate with OpenStack Neutron plugin.

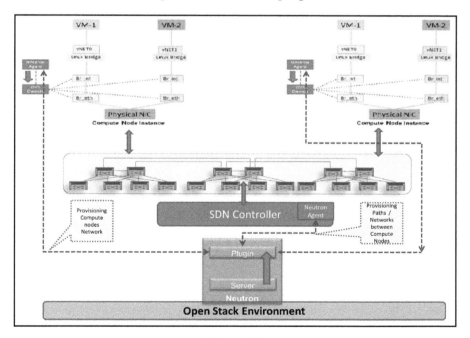

Figure 8.9
End to End view

Putting everything together, here the Neutron plugin will work with upper layer of OpenStack using API, and on the other side it will work with the Neutron agent of the SDN controller. So two operations will happen separately:

- Neutron plugin will work with compute node to give proper IPs and vLANs, etc.

- Neutron plugin will work with the SDN controller by having the path configured between VMs, so communication can happen.

Note that in this figure, the SDN controller is only controlling the switches – which may not be true in many vendor cases. Some SDN controllers do support the VM and swicth controlability from single platform (in SDN language it is known as Overlays and Underlays), if the controller supports overlays and underlays then in that case this figure will change a bit, as in that case the controller controls both the VMs and Networks.

Chapter -9 | OpenStack – Tying Together: Provisioning of VM

Use Case for OpenStack – How a VM is Provisioned

In earlier chapters the focus was more on the component details of the OpenStack and on how each component works. Even if all the components work as designed, a complex set of actions is needed to have a VM provisioned successfully. This chapter explains how the VM is provisioned when a user gives a command via Horizon.

Figure 9.1 explains a reference OpenStack block which is involved in making a VM. On a closer look – you can see pretty much all OpenStack blocks pretty much all blocks of OpenStack are touched when a VM is provisioned (except Swift – which is used for all different usage of storage).

The chapter will have the same recurring figure with the communication links between different modules; there will be explanations given on those steps.

The explanation is given in 14 steps which start with a user requesting for provisioning a VM, and it ends with having a successful notification back to the user.

This chapter gives the steps based on Grizzly release.

Each block presented in figure-9.has been explained in earlier chapters, however, one liner description is given below for all the blocks:

1. Nova – Computing as a service module

2. Compute Node – Instances of Compute nodes

3. Horizon – The GUI, from where a VM can be initiated or deleted.

4. Keystone – Module to do authentication and authorization

5. Cinder – Provide volume service to VM's made in Compute nodes

6. Network Node – Runs as part of controller and provides all networking information needed.

7. Swift – Provides object storage, in some cases it provides repository for Glance (not needed in VM provisioning)

8. Glance – Image as a service, works as a catalogue for providing images to VMs.

9. Neutron – Networking module which works with Network node to give Networking aliments.

With all these components, this chapter explains what happens when a VM is provisioned.

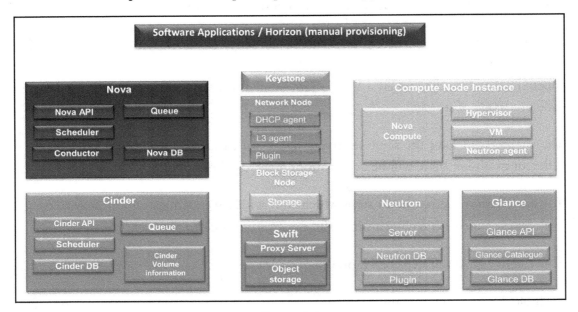

Figure 9.1
The conceptual block diagram of OpenStack

1. Getting the request from Horizon and get it authenticated

In this section, the following steps are taken:

Step 0:

Horizon sends the HTTP authentication requests to Keystone via REST APIs. The authentication information is specified in HTTP header. Keystone looks at the HTTP header and replies with authentication token, which will be used for communicating with other components.

Step 1:

Once Horizon has the authentication token for the user who is requesting for the VM, it contacts Nova API using REST APIs, for making that particular VM.

Step 2:

Using REST APIs, Nova API sends the authentication token to Keystone and Keystone replies within the HTTP header with what roles and authorization are permissible with that authentication token.

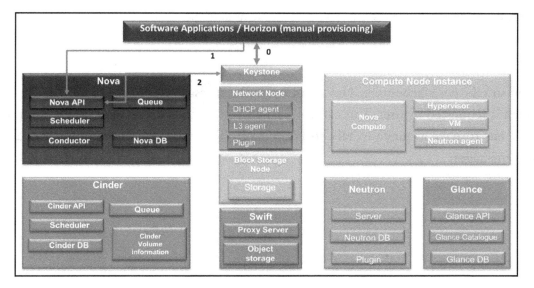

Figure 9.2

2. Nova looks at its data base and writes message in queue

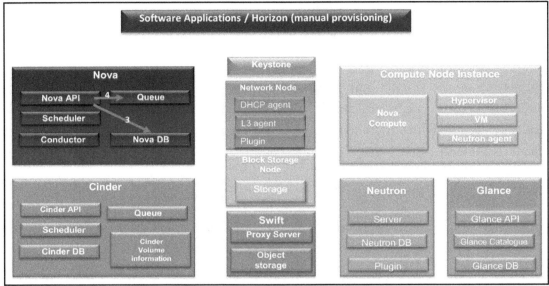

Figure 9.3

Step 3:

Nova will parse the VM creation information with Python parser and if the information is right, it will write the initial information to Nova data base using SQL language.

Step 4:

Now to talk with Scheduler, Nova will write the message in Nova Queue for the VM which is requested by user. This call will be RPC call to the Nova Queue (every compute node has to have a queue to talk to Nova API). This message is communicated using MQ messages.

3. Nova Scheduler comes into the picture and finds out on which host VM will be made:

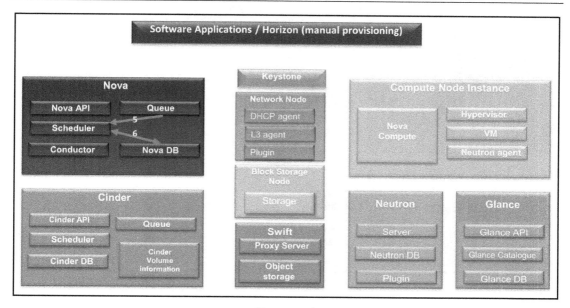

Figure 9.4

Step 5:

Scheduler will pick up the message from Queue. There is a constant polling for the message queue running, wherein different blocks look for any message for them in the queue. How fast the message can be polled, having multiple queue dedicated to each block are all implementation specific. As this communication is happening from AMQP, this will use the MQ messages to communicate.

Step 6:

Scheduler now contacts Nova DB to know which host had how many VMs, to understand weight and load on different hosts. Different filtering and scheduling algorithms can be used to manipulate scheduler to select a particular host for the VM. By this step, scheduler is having the information on which host should have the VM. The communication is done by a SQL language.

4. Scheduler writes the information in Nova queue

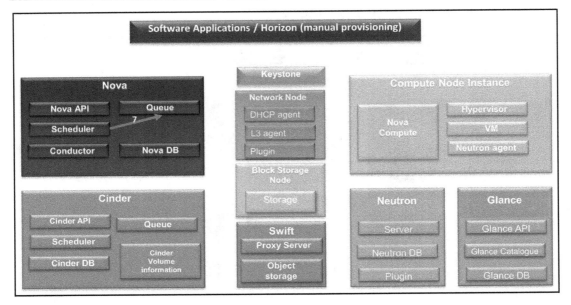

Figure 9.5

Step 7:

Scheduler gets information on the status of current machines and the loads active on those machineS. With that information, Scheduler will decide on which physical node the VM should be provisioned. Once the decision is made, the scheduler will write the message in AMQP using the MQ messages; this message will be for the compute node where the VM should be provisioned.

Note: Different kind of scheduling algorithms have been discussed in previous chapters.

5. Nova works with compute node to start provisioning the VM

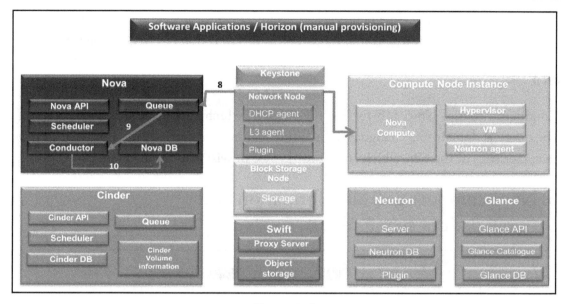

Figure 9.6

Step 8:

As mentioned in previous steps, all the blocks in OpenStack should keep on polling the message queue to get any message, Nova compute nodes follow the same rule and keep polling the Nova controller queue. Eventually it gets the message to provision a VM on that particular compute node.

This communication happens via MQ messages.

In the same step (as per diagram), in reply, Nova compute writes a message back in queue that it wants the properties of the VM to be created. This message is for reading the information from the Nova DB. This message is destined for Nova conductor, not directly for Nova DB. This communication is done in MQ messages.

Note: Nova DB cannot be accessed directly from outside Nova. To get the information from DB, the communication should happen via conductor.

Step 9:

Nova conductor polling the queue gets the message from the queue to contact Nova DB and get the required information. The communication is done in MQ messages.

Step 10:

Conductor queries Nova DB for the information which should be in DB from step 3. The query is done in SQL language. The information is taken from the DB regarding the characteristics of the VM which is supposed to be provisioned by the user.

6. Nova compute gets all information back (reply path of step 8 to 10)

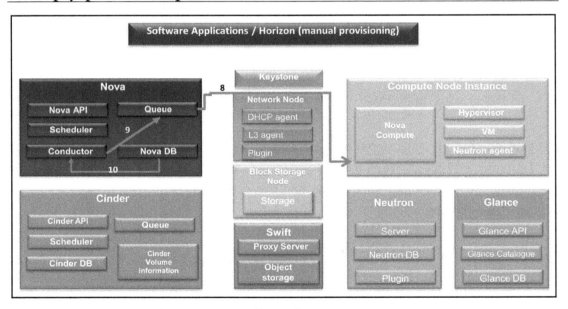

Figure 9.7

Note: Following steps are the reply process of step 8 to 10.

Step 10 (a)

Nova DB provides all information for VM instance to conductor, this reply happens in SQL language.

Step 9 (a)

Conductor writes the information in message queue, so Nova compute node can read it. The message is destined towards the specific compute node which asked for this information. The messaging is done in the form of MQ messages.

Step 8 (a)

Nova compute node reads the information from message queue, and gets all information required for provisioning a VM (CPU, RAM, etc.)

By the end of this step the Nova compute node has the required information on what kind of VM has to be provisioned.

7. Nova computer works with Neutron to get networks information

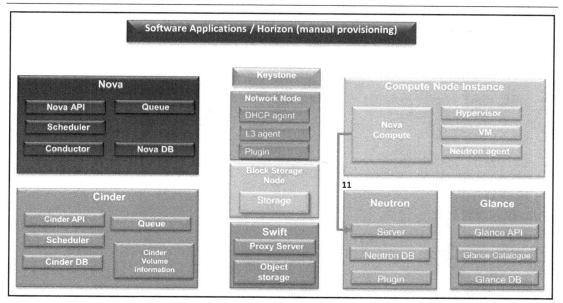

Figure 9.8

Step 11:

Nova compute contacts Neutron server for having networking elements in the VM. Networking element contains IP address, VLAN information, etc. It uses REST APIs to communicate with Neutron server. The neutron server will have server daemon, the Neutron DB (which keeps all records of the networks of the VM), and it will have the plugin. The plugin is the vendor specific code, which may be configured on Neutron server so the APIs can be used to configure vendor specific flows. The exact way how Neutron server will act after getting the request from Nova compute depends upon how the plugin is implemented.

The Neutron server runs on the same node as controller. The network node can run separately; however it runs on controller itself in many scenarios.

8. Neutron works within the module to get all required information for VM provisioning

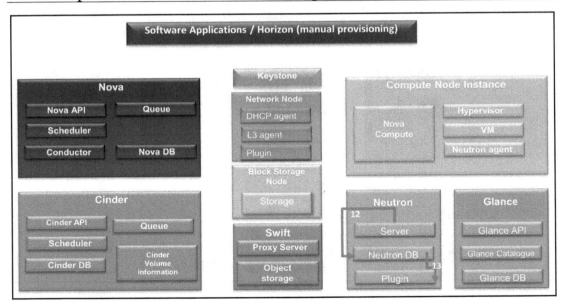

Figure 9.9

Step 12:

Neutron server writes the VM information on Neutron DB. This communication is done using SQL language. The DB will keep the information on which VM is being provisioned and what are the networking related variables it has.

Step 13:

Neutron DB passes the information to Neutron plugin; the information contains the character of VM in terms of networking. As mentioned, the plugin can be residing on the Neutron server (the controller), or on the network node. For this use case example, the plugin is shown in both server and in network node – it may be present in both, or may be only on network node. It depends upon the user implementation.

Wherever it resides, its main job is to talk to the vendor networking appliances (router, switches, firewall, etc.) to configure them according to the needed characteristics provided by Neutron server.

9. Neutron relays all information back to Nova compute

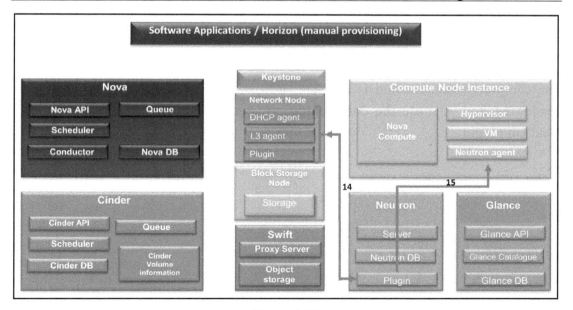

Figure 9.10

Step 14:

Neutron plugin talks to Network node module of OpenStack, this module (network node) runs different agents like the L3 agent for giving the gateway functionality and the DHCP agent for providing the IPs to the newly made VMs. In some vendor plugin implementations, there may be some portion of plugin that would be running on network node as well.

In this step, the main task is to get the variable set (like the IP and the gateway), so it can be fed back to the Neutron/ server and so on to the Nova compute.

The communication method is not standardized here, because it's up to the plugin vendor on how it made the communication channel between different modules of Neutron plugin.

Step 15:

In most of the Neutron plugins there is an agent code which runs on the compute node. This is the agent which configures the VM NIC for the type of connectivity required. The agent typically talks to the Neutron plugin (which is running on controller (neutron server), or on network node – or on both). The plugin agent which runs on the compute node, typically talks to the OVS module and overrides the br_int and br_ext configurations to support different flavors of networks.

The communication method is not standardized here, because it's up to the plugin vendor on how it made the communication channel between different modules of Neutron plugin.

10. Nova compute gets object storage volume from Cinder

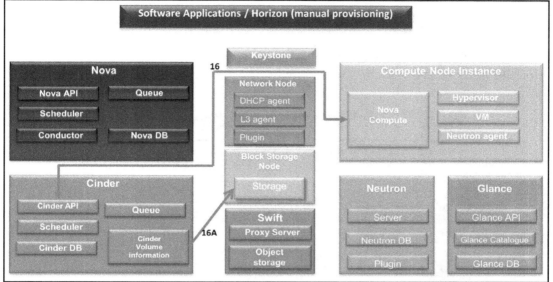

Figure 9.11

Step 16:

This step is optional, as it depends upon whether or not a volume service is needed? The volume as a service provides a persistent storage for a VM instance.

Cinder as a module generally sits on the same machine as does the controller.

In the operation to attach a volume with the VM, Nova compute node contacts Cinder for getting volume attached to the VM. The storage can be attached after VM is created. iSCSI types of storages are used for block storage.

This communication between nova compute and Cinder API is done via RESTfull APIs.

Step 16A:

This step is an overview step on what happens after step 16. After the Nova compute contacts Cinder API for providing a volume for Block storage, the Cinder API internally talks to the scheduler to know which Block storage is free. Once the decision is made, the Cinder Volume information will talk to Block storage node (black storage is typically iSCSI storage). The communication between Cinder and the Block storage is done via vendor's proprietary protocols.

Once the Block storage is reserved for the VM, the Nova compute will have all the information on where to locate the volume for the provisioned VM.

11. Nova compute now attaches the Block storage

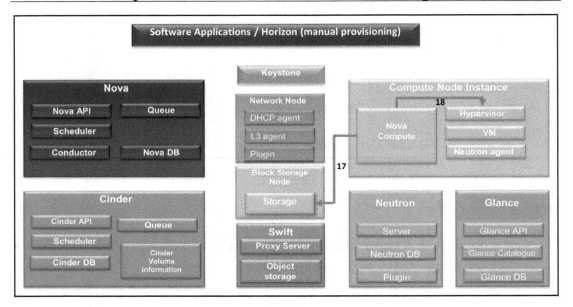

Figure 9.12

Step 17:

Nova compute node gets the Block storage information from Block storage node, the Nova compute communicates with Block storage with iSCSI language. Block storage is the persistent data of the VM.

Step 18:

After having all the information on Black storage, the Nova compute sends the signal to Hypervisor to mount the block storage as a volume for the VM. Compute node now mounts Hypervisor with Block storage iSCSI target.

12. Nova compute now gets the image from Glance

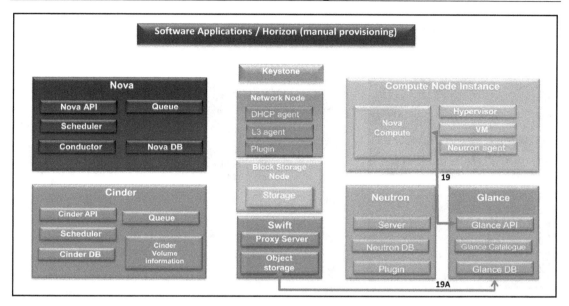

Figure 9.13

Step 19:

Now as the compute node has the information ready for networking, and it has the information for the volume, it needs an image to boot the VM. In this step, Nova compute accesses Glance API using Rest API to get the image for the VM.

Glance is typically installed on the same machine as the controller. However, the real image can be stored on the attached storage or in the Swift component. Glance itself is basically just a catalogue of images.

Step 19A:

Once the Glance API gets the request for getting the image for VM, the Glance catalogue finds the line item and Glance DB gives the information to access the real image, which can be sent to Nova compute to have the VM initiated. The real image can be stored on Swift (as shown in this example), the image can also be stored on the attached storage device on the machine where Glance is running.

13. Nova is updated with the newly made VM

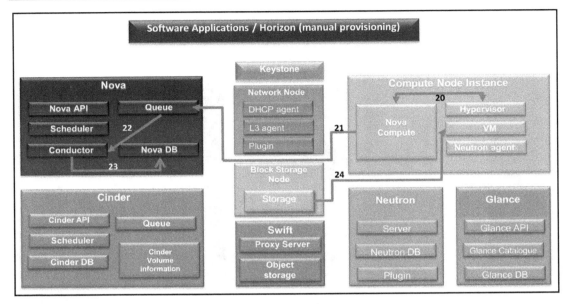

Figure 9.14

Step 20 & 24:

Till step 19, Nova compute has all the information needed to provision a VM. In the steps after 19, the compute node provisions the VM on the Hypervisor, using the volume service in Block storage.

Step 21:

While the VM is provisioned, the Nova compute should update the Nova DB, so that it communicates with Nova queue that VM is functional. This information should be sent so that the DB has information about the load of the compute node, and also the details of VM – so it can be rolled back to the user GUI, etc. The communication is done using MQ message.

Step 22:

Conductor reads from Nova queue and it reads the information which instructs it to write the information into Nova DB.

Step 23:

Conductor updates the Nova DB with the VM information.

14. Nova reports back to Horizon

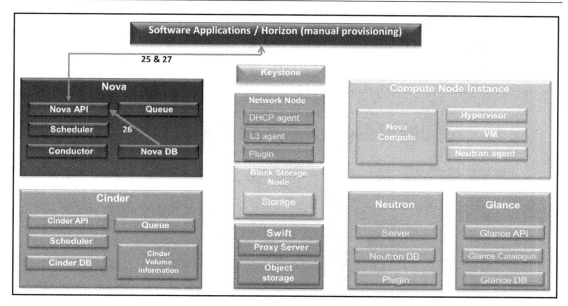

Figure 9.15

Step 25:

While all the steps from 1 to 24 are happening, the Horizon keeps on polling the information on the newly asked VM. Various states of VM provisioning can be seen on Horizon GUI, while it polls for the state of VM.

Step 26:

Upon getting a poll from Horizon, Nova API polls the DB to find out if it has the final state of the VM. This operation keeps on happening -- so if step 24 has happened, the Nova API will get the information in this DB.

Step 27:

Nova API reports the state of VM to Horizon and the provisioned VM can be seen in Horizon GUI.

End-to-end Deployment of OpenStack

The previous sections of this chapter went into details of how the VM is provisioned. Provisioning a VM is one use case of the OpenStack. Figure 9.20 gives the details of how end-to-end OpenStack deployment will look like.

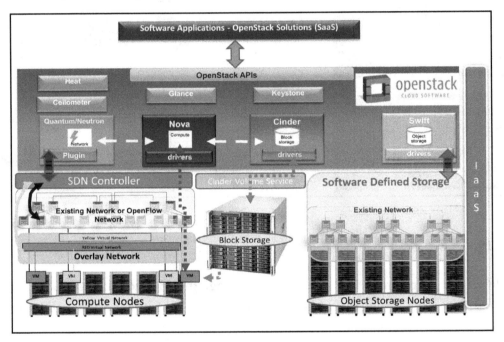

Figure 9.20
End-to-end deployment of OpenStack

This is the same diagram as given in Chapter 2. As explained, the OpenStack oversees the entire hardware which is deployed in the data center. On the networking side, the SDN (or normal) controller will talk to the switches (underlay) and overlays made for VMs. There are many SDN companies working in this space to bring the network commodity in this space – wherein all intelligence will run in SDN controller and the network hardware is treated as commodity.

On the Block storage side (which provides the volume services), it will interact with vendor plugin (may be known as Cinder Volume Service) and deploy the Block storages for the VMs.

In the diagram, the Swift is separate and talking to Object storage nodes. There is a new technology coming up in that area of Cloud, which is known as Software Defined Storage (SDS). The idea of SDS is to virtualize the storage and bring all the intelligence in software controller – keeping real hardware as a commodity. There are many start-ups working on that domain.

Chapter -10 | Havana – Heat & Ceilometer

Havana release

It is the eighth release of OpenStack and was released in October 2013. This is the latest release as of now, and supports the same charter of OpenStack – to be the Cloud operating system for public, private and hybrid Cloud.

Every incremental release comes with numerous bug fixes and also new features which make the deployment more robust and hence takes it one more step nearer to more install base.

In Havana release, there are two new services:

- Orchestration service   : Heat
- Metering Service : Ceilometer

This chapter explains these two services.

Heat

What is Heat

Heat is the OpenStack project which is pushing for orchestration of Cloud infrastructure. In Heat, the orchestration can be done by defining the templates and introducing the concept of stacks. As of now, in Havana the template is still evolving, so for now the well-established template is defined for AWS (Amazon Web Services) users.

How heat works

Heat works on template basis; a template defines the infrastructure for a Cloud application. The definition is in the form of code file written and managed by Cloud admins. The components of infrastructure are servers, storages, networks, etc. The template defines the basic component needed for a Cloud application, and it also defines the relation between those components. By defining the template like this, a full system can be provisioned quickly and because the definition is defined in template, the on-demand scaling can be done (the term is known as auto-scaling).

Components of Heat

The diagram explains the basic components of Heat. As explained in the diagram, there are two types of APIs which can feed the template in heat system:

• Native Heat APIs

• AWS based APIs

Once the template definition is in the Heat system, the Rabbit queue will feed this into the Heat engine. The Heat engine will process the template and work with different modules of OpenStack to provision the stack on-demand (by auto-scaling, etc.). The Head Data Base will keep the information of templates and what is provisioned.

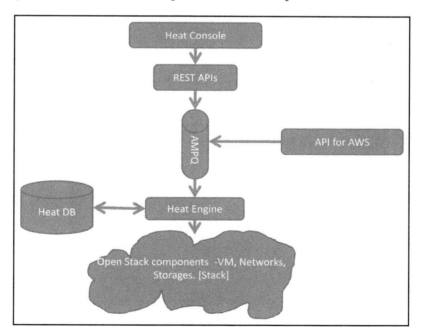

Figure 10.1
Overview of Heat

Types of Templates -

- CNF Cloud Formation Template

This template is used by AWS. Heat provides a way to use these templates in OpenStack environment.

- HOT (Heat Orchestration Template) Template

This is a native template being developed for Heat OpenStack. Functionally, it will be the same as AWS templates. This template is still evolving.

Concept of Stack in Heat

The stack is defined as a group of servers, networks, storage (volumes), etc, and the relation between these components. By Heat, a stack template can be defined and that template can be used to provision different flavours of stack (by passing different set of configurations).

Ceilometer

What is Ceilometer

With OpenStack getting deployed in Cloud, there is a need to have a proper billing and usage monitoring service. Ceilometer provides the billing and monitoring service, working in tandem with all OpenStack components and compute nodes, especially. The monitoring happens on the polling basis as well as on event trigger basis.

Ceilometer is not tightly coupled with the component layer of OpenStack – this gives it the flexibility to measure the usage at Iaas, Paas or at Saas layers.

How Ceilometer works

Ceilometer exposes the RESTfull APIs which can be used to define the billing and usage system. Once the upper layer accesses the Ceilometer via RESTfull APIs, it will be saved in the data base. The collector will poll the data base and will know if there is any new poll request came in. If there is any poll request, the collector will start polling the usage of different modules and compute nodes via event queue. There is a mechanism for modules to give information on any event if that happens between polling.

Components of Ceilometer

The diagram explains the basic components of Ceilometer. As explained in the diagram, these are the following components of Ceilometer:

•   Data base

Data base keeps information of all billing and usage requests. It could be any data base which keeps track of Ceilometer data. The main requirement is to have support for sequential reads and writes.

•   REST APIs

This is the public face of the Ceilometer where it contacts user applications and gets the request and gives back the response.

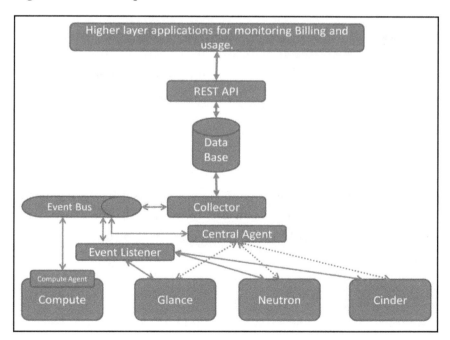

Figure 10.2
Overview of Ceilometer

- Compute Agent

This agent runs on compute node and will poll for the data on the utilization of resources (resources used by VMs, the traffic utilization, etc.).

- Central Agent

A central agent runs on central controller where Ceilometer is installed, it polls from all components of OpenStack.

- Collector

This component runs on the central controller where Ceilometer is installed, and it collects all the information on usage from Event Bus and in some cases from the central agent.

- Oslo event Bus listener

The generated events are sent on the Oslo notification Bus and the Event Bus translates this data in to sample which can be consumed by Ceilometer collector.

Publishing of data

Once the collector has the data, it can be accessed from the database and can be published using RESTfull APIs.

Concept of Alarm

Ceilometer comes with a facility for triggering an alarm based on the sampled data. A Cloud administrator can define the trigger point and the polling from the data base, when the conditions are met – the alarm can be triggered. The alarm can be used to automate the auto-scaling or could be used as a trigger point to stop scaling or to start/ stop any application.

Chapter -11 | OpenStack – Simple Configuration Example

This chapter is dedicated to give cookie-cutter configurations for an OpenStack setup. The topology used in this use case is a multi-node – which means is that there are two compute nodes and VM can sit on any of the compute node.

In figure 11.1, the first compute node (CN-1) is residing on the same physical machine where the controller is installed. The second compute node (CN-2) is a separate physical server. On the networks side, two networks can be seen. The 192.x network is the management network, which pretty much used for all OpenStack communications. The network 80.x is the network used as real network connections for data path.

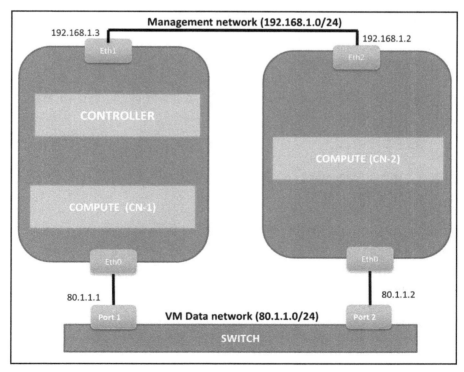

Figure 11.1 (Use case deployment for OpenStack).

For connectivity between the compute nodes, the switch is connected, which is connecting two compute nodes. For simplicity, the switch is configured in a single VLAN. The switch can be configured by a SDN controller too depends upon the specific deployments.

On the compute node the OVS network plugin has been taken in this example. The OVS plugin will do the networking part on the compute nodes. If there a network plugin from some other vendor the networking side configurations may change a bit.

Multi-node OpenStack configuration using PackStack with Flat networking

Step -1: Pre configurations on Controller (and CN-1)

- Run the following command to install OpenStack on a single node using PackStack utility. This utility will install most of the required configuration for controller and compute node CN-1.

Packstack —allinone

Step-2: Pre-configurations to add compute node 2 (CN-2)

- Rerun PackStack on the controller with the following changes in the PackStack-answer-file:

  * *change CONFIG_NOVA_COMPUTE_PRIVIF from lo to eth0*
  * change CONFIG_NOVA_COMPUTE_HOSTS by replacing IP to 192.168.1.2 (compute node IP)

After installation is complete, verify on the controller with 'nova service-list' command to see two compute node from different hosts are enabled as highlighted below.

(In below example openstkcmpt215 and openstkcntr213 are two different nodes)

```
[root@openstkcmpt215 ~(keystone_admin)]# nova service-list
+-----------------+----------------+----------+----------+-------+----------------------------+-----------------+
| Binary          | Host           | Zone     | Status   | State | Updated_at                 | Disabled Reason |
+-----------------+----------------+----------+----------+-------+----------------------------+-----------------+
| nova-consoleauth| openstkcmpt215 | internal | enabled  | up    | 2014-01-28T06:15:19.000000 | None            |
| nova-scheduler  | openstkcmpt215 | internal | enabled  | up    | 2014-01-28T06:15:21.000000 | None            |
| nova-conductor  | openstkcmpt215 | internal | enabled  | up    | 2014-01-28T06:15:18.000000 | None            |
| nova-cert       | openstkcmpt215 | internal | enabled  | up    | 2014-01-28T06:15:18.000000 | None            |
| nova-compute    | openstkcmpt215 | nova     | enabled  | up    | 2014-01-28T06:15:18.000000 | None            |
| nova-compute    | openstkcntr213 | nova     | enabled  | up    | 2014-01-28T06:15:18.000000 | None            |
| nova-console    | openstkcmpt215 | internal | enabled  | up    | 2014-01-28T06:15:19.000000 | None            |
+-----------------+----------------+----------+----------+-------+----------------------------+-----------------+
```

Step-3: Additional configurations on Controller physical server (includes Compute node CN-1)

• Modify the OpenStack networking configuration file on controller, /etc/neutron/neutron.conf to set controller IP for the rabbit host used to implement AMQP between controller and compute.

```
# SSL version to use (valid only if SSL enabled)
# kombu_ssl_version =
# SSL key file (valid only if SSL enabled)
# kombu_ssl_keyfile =
# SSL cert file (valid only if SSL enabled)
# kombu_ssl_certfile =
# SSL certification authority file (valid only if SSL enabled)'
# kombu_ssl_ca_certs =
# IP address of the RabbitMQ installation
rabbit_host = <Controller IP>
# Password of the RabbitMQ server
# rabbit_password = guest
# Port where RabbitMQ server is running/listening
# rabbit_port = 5672
```

• Modify the plugin configuration file on controller, /etc/neutron/plugins/openvswitch/ovs_neutron_plugin.ini -

This uses VLAN isolation on the switches to isolate tenant networks. This configuration labels the physical network associated with the public network as physnet1

```
# [database]
# connection = mysql://root:nova@127.0.0.1:3306/ovs_neutron
[ovs]
# tunnel_id_ranges =
#enable_tunneling=False
# integration_bridge = br-int
tenant_network_type = vlan
network_vlan_ranges = physnet1:2000:3999
bridge_mappings = physnet1:br-eth0
# [AGENT]
```

- Create a network bridge br-eth0 on controller – for VM communication between nodes via eth0:

sudo ovs-vsctl add-br br-eth0

sudo ovs-vsctl add-port br-eth0 eth0

- Modify the compute node CN-1 config on controller, /etc/nova/nova.conf

When nova-compute creates an instance, it must 'plug' each of the instance's vNICs into an OpenStack Network controlled virtual switch, and inform the virtual switch about the OpenStack Network port-id associated with each vNIC. We indicate this in nova.conf that we need Vif-plugging with Open vSwitch Plugin

```
#libvirt_vif_driver=nova.virt.libvirt.vif.LibvirtGenericVIFDriver
libvirt_vif_driver=nova.virt.libvirt.vif.LibvirtHybridOVSBridgeDriver
```

- Restart OpenStack networking, Compute and plugin services on controller.

Step-4: Configuration of Compute node CN-2:

- Modify the openstack networking configuration file on compute node CN-2, /etc/neutron/neutron.conf to set controller IP for the rabbit host.

```
# SSL version to use (valid only if SSL enabled)
# kombu_ssl_version =
# SSL key file (valid only if SSL enabled)
# kombu_ssl_keyfile =
# SSL cert file (valid only if SSL enabled)
# kombu_ssl_certfile =
# SSL certification authority file (valid only if SSL enabled)'
# kombu_ssl_ca_certs =
# IP address of the RabbitMQ installation
rabbit_host = <Controller IP>
# Password of the RabbitMQ server
# rabbit_password = guest
# Port where RabbitMQ server is running/listening
# rabbit_port = 5672
```

- Modify the plugin configuration file on compute node CN-2 to change it into flat vlan network, /etc/neutron/plugins/openvswitch/ovs_neutron_plugin.ini:

```
# [database]
# connection = mysql://root:nova@127.0.0.1:3306/ovs_neutron
[ovs]
# tunnel_id_ranges =
#enable_tunneling=False
# integration_bridge = br-int
tenant_network_type = vlan
network_vlan_ranges = physnet1:2000:3999
bridge_mappings = physnet1:br-eth0
# [AGENT]
```

- Create a network bridge br-eth0 on compute node CN-2– for VM communication between nodes via eth0:

sudo ovs-vsctl add-br br-eth0
sudo ovs-vsctl add-port br-eth0 eth0

- Modify the compute node CN-2 config on compute node CN-2 to use openvswitch plugin, /etc/nova/nova.conf

```
#libvirt_vif_driver=nova.virt.libvirt.vif.LibvirtGenericVIFDriver
libvirt_vif_driver=nova.virt.libvirt.vif.LibvirtHybridOVSBridgeDriver
```

- Restart openstack networking, Compute and plugin services on compute node CN-2

Step-5: Create a flat network on controller

- [root@openstkcmpt215 init.d]# source keystonerc_admin

- Get the tenant ID. To get the admin Tenant ID:

```
[root@openstkcmpt215 init.d(keystone_admin)]# keystone tenant-list
+----------------------------------+----------+---------+
|                id                |   name   | enabled |
+----------------------------------+----------+---------+
| fb3ec2d4851444c9924dd81de14bbf00 |  admin   |  True   |
| f15eae852dc440e1a616912ba868720d | alt_demo |  True   |
| 6df2107942c34083bde846fef4d3fbf6 |   demo   |  True   |
| 35f6b1b1d8b249f4a45d1bb33f9c17bf | services |  True   |
+----------------------------------+----------+---------+
```

- Here an internal shared network is created using admin tenant

(admin $tenant_ID: fb3ec2d4851444c9924dd81de14bbf00)

```
[root@openstkcmpt215 init.d(keystone_admin)]# neutron net-create --tenant-id fb3ec2d4
851444c9924dd81de14bbf00 sharednet --shared --provider:network_type flat --provider:p
hysical_network physnet1
Created a new network:
+-----------------------------+------------------------------------------+
| Field                       | Value                                    |
+-----------------------------+------------------------------------------+
| admin_state_up              | True                                     |
| id                          | cbb1f4c6-d1ae-4456-96d0-53d22f009e66     |
| name                        | sharednet                                |
| provider:network_type       | flat                                     |
| provider:physical_network   | physnet1                                 |
| provider:segmentation_id    |                                          |
| shared                      | True                                     |
| status                      | ACTIVE                                   |
| subnets                     |                                          |
| tenant_id                   | fb3ec2d4851444c9924dd81de14bbf00         |
+-----------------------------+------------------------------------------+
```

- Create a subnet for shared network

```
[root@openstkcmpt215 init.d(keystone_admin)]# neutron subnet-create --tenant-id fb3ec
2d4851444c9924dd81de14bbf00 sharednet 80.0.0.0/24
Created a new subnet:
+-------------------+----------------------------------------------+
| Field             | Value                                        |
+-------------------+----------------------------------------------+
| allocation_pools  | {"start": "80.0.0.2", "end": "80.0.0.254"}   |
| cidr              | 80.0.0.0/24                                   |
| dns_nameservers   |                                              |
| enable_dhcp       | True                                         |
| gateway_ip        | 80.0.0.1                                     |
| host_routes       |                                              |
| id                | ffeb5bcc-ff3f-4cfc-bffd-452f4e221381         |
| ip_version        | 4                                            |
| name              |                                              |
| network_id        | cbb1f4c6-d1ae-4456-96d0-53d22f009e66         |
| tenant_id         | fb3ec2d4851444c9924dd81de14bbf00             |
+-------------------+----------------------------------------------+
```

Step-6: Check the image installed required for VM instances

```
[root@openstkcmpt215 init.d(keystone_admin)]# nova image-list
+--------------------------------------+--------+--------+--------+
| ID                                   | Name   | Status | Server |
+--------------------------------------+--------+--------+--------+
| ac8779b7-2c31-4d48-92f9-5afa3b626cca | cirros | ACTIVE |        |
+--------------------------------------+--------+--------+--------+
```

Step-7: Launch a VM instance from terminal (it can also be done from dashboard)

```
[root@openstkcmpt215 ~(keystone_admin)]# nova boot --image ac8779b7-2c31-4d48-92f9-5afa3b626c
ca --flavor 1 --nic net-id=cbb1f4c6-d1ae-4456-96d0-53d22f009e66 --availability-zone nova:open
stkcmpt215 vm3_admin
+-------------------------------------+--------------------------------------+
| Property                            | Value                                |
+-------------------------------------+--------------------------------------+
| OS-EXT-STS:task_state               | scheduling                           |
| image                               | cirros                               |
| OS-EXT-STS:vm_state                 | building                             |
| OS-EXT-SRV-ATTR:instance_name       | instance-00000003                    |
| OS-SRV-USG:launched_at              | None                                 |
| flavor                              | m1.tiny                              |
| id                                  | 5140250b-e882-43fe-8999-97686fbda9cb |
| security_groups                     | [{u'name': u'default'}]              |
| user_id                             | 71a6060f46b34cbca8e5e52f6b1b49b1     |
| OS-DCF:diskConfig                   | MANUAL                               |
| accessIPv4                          |                                      |
| accessIPv6                          |                                      |
| progress                            | 0                                    |
| OS-EXT-STS:power_state              | 0                                    |
| OS-EXT-AZ:availability_zone         | nova                                 |
| config_drive                        |                                      |
| status                              | BUILD                                |
| updated                             | 2014-01-29T00:09:58Z                 |
| hostId                              |                                      |
| OS-EXT-SRV-ATTR:host                | None                                 |
| OS-SRV-USG:terminated_at            | None                                 |
| key_name                            | None                                 |
| OS-EXT-SRV-ATTR:hypervisor_hostname | None                                 |
| name                                | vm3_admin                            |
| adminPass                           | sejaXAgE679h                         |
| tenant_id                           | fb3ec2d4851444c9924dd81de14bbf00     |
| created                             | 2014-01-29T00:09:58Z                 |
| os-extended-volumes:volumes_attached| []                                   |
| metadata                            | {}                                   |
+-------------------------------------+--------------------------------------+
```

Step-8: Check the VM instance status on terminal

```
[root@openstkcmpt215 ~(keystone_admin)]# nova list
+--------------------------------------+-----------+--------+------------+-------------+----------------------+
| ID                                   | Name      | Status | Task State | Power State | Networks             |
+--------------------------------------+-----------+--------+------------+-------------+----------------------+
| f8d3219a-f201-4f3e-ab13-a29be14880d5 | vm1_admin | ACTIVE | None       | Running     | sharednet=80.0.0.2   |
| fe450dcc-0251-41a0-b418-9b9ffa476f06 | vm2_admin | ACTIVE | None       | Running     | sharednet=80.0.0.4   |
| 5140250b-e882-43fe-8999-97686fbda9cb | vm3_admin | ACTIVE | None       | Running     | sharednet=80.0.0.5   |
+--------------------------------------+-----------+--------+------------+-------------+----------------------+
[root@openstkcmpt215 ~(keystone_admin)]#
```

Step-9: Check the VM status on controller dashboard

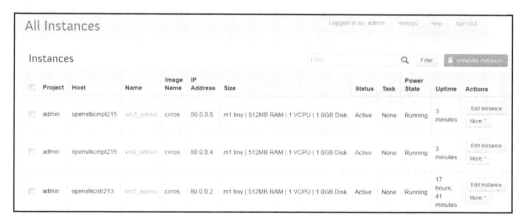

Bibliography

- http://ken.pepple.info/OpenStack/2011/04/22/OpenStack-nova-architecture/

- https://www.ibm.com/developerworks/community/blogs/e93514d3-c4f0-4aa0-8844-497f370090f5/entry/OpenStack_nova_api?lang=en

- https://www.ibm.com/developerworks/community/blogs/e93514d3-c4f0-4aa0-8844-497f370090f5/entry/OpenStack_nova_scheduler_and_its_algorithm27?lang=en

- http://docs.OpenStack.org/folsom/OpenStack-compute/admin/content/adding-images.html

- http://docs.OpenStack.org/trunk/OpenStack-image-service/admin/content/overview-of-glance-architecture.html

- http://docs.OpenStack.org/developer/swift/overview_architecture.html

- https://wiki.OpenStack.org/wiki/Neutron

- http://docs.openstack.org/trunk/openstack-etwork/admin/content/use_cases_single_flat.html

- http://docs.openstack.org/trunk/openstack-network/admin/content/use_cases_single_flat.html

- Software Defined Storage (with OpenStack Swift) – by Joe Arnold

- OpenStack – by Ken Peppel

- Cloud computing concepts, technology & architecture – by Thomas Erl, Zaighan, Ricardo

www.ingramcontent.com/pod-product-compliance
Lightning Source LLC
Chambersburg PA
CBHW060450060326
40689CB00020B/4482